Communicating With Clients: A Guide for Financial Professionals

Charles J. Pulvino,
James L. Lee, and
Cynthia E. Forman

Communicating With Clients: A Guide for Financial Professionals

Charles J. Pulvino,
James L. Lee, and
Cynthia E. Forman

Prentice Hall Information Services
Paramus, NJ 07652

Contents

Preface

We are aware of the need for facilitative communication skills. We see this need not only in our daily interactions but more importantly in our encounters with professional financial counselors and financial planners. We have previously applied interviewing skills to the financial counseling process and the financial planning process. In this book, we have focused our efforts on effective communication skills for professionals working in a variety of financial settings. We have expanded our earlier thoughts on interviewing and broadened our view of communication.

We believe that professionals in financial services can use this book as a map for effective communication because it considers both basic and advanced communication skills. Skills are presented in a way that reflects the unique relationship that exists between financial professionals and their clients. We believe that effective communication skills, always beneficial in daily life, take on added significance when applied in situations that revolve around the management of personal resources.

It is our intention that the reader be given a chance to think about concepts, to see how they are applied, and to practice their use. With that end in mind, we discuss principles, share positive interactions, highlight practical examples, and provide opportunities for practicing the ideas presented. To the degree we were successful in our efforts, the reader will be a more informed communicator and ultimately a more efficient, effective financial professional.

JLL
CJP
CEF

Prologue:

A Real-Life Example of Poor Communication

Picture the following scene that occurred between one of the authors and a car salesman. The last child was moving off to college and Dad was interested in buying a new sports car, something he had owned before the children started driving. He had stopped to look at a new Mazda RX-7 and was examining one sitting on the lot.

Salesman (approaching from the salesroom): It's a real honey, isn't it?

Dad: Yes, I've always liked the styling of the RX-7.

Salesman: Well, we've got some real good deals right now. Have you looked at any other sports cars?

Dad: Yes, I've looked at the Corvette, but that's way beyond my budget. I've also been looking at the new Pontiac Fiero GT and I'm really impressed with it.

Salesman: Well, there's no comparison between the RX-7 and the Fiero. The Mazda is twice the car the Fiero is.

Dad: Why do you say that?

Salesman: Well, in the first place the RX-7 has the rotary engine, which gives it much more power. It acts like a sports car is supposed to act. The Fiero just looks like a sports car but doesn't have any power.

Dad: Well, I don't know; the new Fiero GT has a fuel injected V-6, and I was really impressed with the power it has.

Salesman: Yeah, but it doesn't have the power this baby sitting here has!

Dad: Have you driven one of the new Fiero GTs?

Salesman: No, I don't have to. This car will outrun any Fiero! Besides, it has a real body, not one of those cheap plastic jobs.

Dad: I thought the plastic body was a plus. I don't need to pay for rustproofing and it won't ever get car cancer.

Salesman: Well, yeah! But who wants a plastic car?

Dad: I might!

Salesman: Well, another thing, this car here has twice as much room as the Fiero!

Dad: It does have more room in the back. The Fiero has two trunks, though. I only need room for my golf clubs and maybe an overnight bag.

Salesman: Yes, but I was referring to passenger space. With a tall guy like you (Dad is 6′2″), you will have a lot more leg room.

Dad: Can I sit in it to see?

Salesman: Sure.

Dad squeezes into the car and puts the seat back as far as it will go. His knees are still against the steering wheel and his head is touching the ceiling of the car. This is in direct contrast to his experience in the Fiero. In the Fiero, with the seat all the way back, he couldn't push the clutch in all the way and there were two inches of clearance above his head.

Salesman: You see—there is plenty of room in there for you.

Dad: No! My knees are against the steering wheel and my head is pushed into the ceiling.

Salesman: Well, I'll bet there is more room than in the Fiero.

Dad: As a matter of fact, I had more room in the Fiero.

Salesman: Yes, but I bet they didn't have a sun roof.

Dad: Yes, it did.

After a few more similar interchanges and by consciously resisting any attempt by the salesman to get him inside to start figuring out what the car would cost, Dad left. When Dad reached his car, where his wife was waiting, he said, "If I ever did buy a Mazda, it wouldn't be from that guy!"

CHAPTER 1

The Foundations of Communication

Lao-Tzo, the Chinese philosopher, once said, "The longest journey begins with but a single step." That important first step in professional communication is the development of an effective communicative relationship between yourself and your clients. The salesman in the prologue obviously got off on the wrong foot! Accomplishing this first step begins with an understanding of the communicative process. In this chapter we will focus on how people process information. Since communication revolves around the transmittal of information, it is important to understand how people process information internally and how information affects the way people behave.

The principles to be covered in this chapter are as follows:

Principle 1.1: There is no best way to communicate.

Principle 1.2: People develop personal representations of experience.

Principle 1.3: People develop preferential ways of processing information.

Principle 1.4: Changing information in one processing mode changes information in other processing modes.

Principle 1.5: The number of choices people have at any point in time is directly related to the amount of detail in their representational maps.

Principle 1.6: People naturally generalize.

Principle 1.7: People process information differentially.

Principle 1.8: People seek informational harmony and closure.

Principle 1.9: People usually do what is best for themselves using stored information.

Principle 1.10: Communicative interactions are reciprocal.

Principle 1.11: The majority of stored information/learning is not conscious.

Every professional relationship depends upon effective communication, whether it is a sales presentation, as in the prologue; an encounter between manager and employee; or a meeting between you and your client. Our goal is to remind you of things you already know about effective communication, to add structure to the relationships you build in your profession, and to show you how to develop the most effective working relationships with your clients.

The Role of Information Processing. The success of your work as a professional usually relies on how well you communicate. You communicate every day, and it seems like a normal and natural process. Few of us consciously decide what to say when we communicate. The thoughts and words just seem to flow. Yet, have you ever thought about how complicated this process is? How do people decide what to communicate? Where do their thoughts and words come from? How can two people experience the same event and communicate two entirely different reactions?

When you begin to examine the process, it becomes apparent that we do many things without consciously thinking about them. We act and react from experience or habit. There are a number of explanations for why we respond as we do. Most explanations involve concepts about how people process information. A number of principles about the way in which people process information can provide us with an understanding of the communicative process.

Principle 1.1: *There is no best way to communicate.* In a book about developing effective communication relationships it may seem odd to begin with a principle that says there is no best way to communicate. The underlying meaning of this principle might be better understood through an example:

Suppose you want to travel from Madison, Wisconsin, to Buffalo, New York. There are an almost infinite variety of means of transportation and routes that can be used. You can get from Madison to Buffalo by train, plane, car, bicycle, and so on. If you are raising money for a charitable organization, you might even walk. If you choose to fly to Buffalo, you can fly directly to Buffalo. You can fly through Chicago. You can even fly to San Francisco, then fly on around the world and back to Buffalo. It is only when you assign certain values and goals to the trip that one route becomes better than another. If efficiency is most important, you will probably choose the most direct flying route. If you are on vacation, and want to relax and experience the various forms of American culture in the process, you probably will drive and make a number of side trips. For example, you could go through Michigan and stop to see how cars are made in Detroit or how chocolate is made in Hershey, Pennsylvania. Each new set of values and goals makes one form of transportation *better* than another.

The same is true of communication. The value system and the goals you have affect the choices you make. You can accomplish your communicative goals in a variety of ways. Some ways become better than others when we apply certain values or have specific goals. For example, psychiatrist Milton Erickson is credited with an anecdote about several dentists who developed an effective way of dealing with children who were so afraid of dentists that they responded with crying, screaming fits when brought into their offices. The dentists wanted to have cooperative patients. They told the children as they arrived that they had nothing to fear. Then the dentists tied towels around the children's mouths and tied them into their chairs. The dentists reported that the children were always very cooperative at their next appointments.

Anyone would be cooperative when they visit the dentist if they knew that otherwise they were going to get their mouths stuffed with towels and their hands tied to the chair. So, in one sense, we can say that the dentists used effective communication because it produced their desired goal. It resulted in cooperative patients.

> ⋙**INEFFECTIVE, TOO!**→ The dentists' system doesn't teach children how to deal with their fear of dentists. They merely learn a new fear on top of an underlying fear. So the same episode shows ineffective communication.

In this book we will apply two underlying values to distinguish effective, professional communication from less effective communication.

▸*Humanistic, growth-producing treatment*. By humanistic and growth-producing, we refer to communication that maximizes a person's own potential and that treats that person as worthwhile.

▸*Efficiency and parsimony*. Effective communication attempts to achieve goals as quickly and effortlessly as possible. So, while one might accomplish the same goal a number of different ways and be humanistic, we think that accomplishing the goal in the most efficient way is better.

Principle 1.2: *People develop personal representations of experience.* As people grow and develop, they store their life experiences and their reactions to those experiences. A person's experiences are gradually woven into a personal representation of the world. These finely woven representations have been called perceptions, tapes, personal rules, and maps. Each person's package of life experiences is analogous to a fine tapestry. New experiences are like new threads. They have an identity of their own, they become woven into the tapestry, and eventually they form a small design which becomes part of the greater design.

In this book we will refer to these finely woven personal representations as *maps*. We believe that people build unique maps of the world because no two people have exactly the same experiences. On the other hand, it is also true that there are many similarities among people and, therefore, among representational maps. For example, most people will have a similar map of the word *table*. When someone mentions a table, we probably form a picture of a four-legged piece of furniture. It may not be exactly the same representation as the person who said the word, but we probably would agree on basic characteristics, for example, a piece of furniture with four legs and a flat top.

As we use abstract words, we probably wouldn't have the same degree of mutual understanding. An abstract word like *fun* will have as many representations as there are people. For example, some people think that running two or three miles a day is *fun*. They enjoy using their body, working up a good sweat, and feeling better about their health. They might say, "Running is fun!" A second group of people might respond in a totally different manner. They might dislike the idea of exerting that much energy or of working up a sweat. They might think that sitting and reading a book is *fun*, and that running or jogging is agony.

> ⋙**MAPS GOVERN BEHAVIOR**→ It is important to realize that behaviors are influenced by individuals' maps. People's maps govern how they behave and, to a large degree, how they think. People who think running is fun will arrange their schedules to engage in this activity. In like manner, people who would rather do something else will arrange their schedules to allow time for their personal *kind of fun*.

An understanding of representational maps provides a basis for understanding two common errors people make, errors which can have a very negative impact on effective communication.

People may assume that their representational maps are the same as reality. Frequently, individuals fail to recognize that their experience is a combination of what their present sensory experience is telling them and what their representational maps allow them to perceive at any point in time.

Individuals may assume that what is true for them must be true for others. In essence, it is very easy for individuals to believe that what they perceive must be what is.

These two errors are the basis for much miscommunication and misunderstanding. In the prologue the salesman had his personal conception of reality, one which he believed would be true of any customer interested in sports cars. He in turn assumed that the customer would share those same representational maps of the world. The salesman's assumption was false, and he lost a potential customer.

The beginning of an effective, professional communicative relationship is the recognition that the client's map of the world is potentially different from yours. An important first step in communication is for you to understand the client's map of the world and how it is similar to and dissimilar from yours. Clients' maps affect how they make decisions; how they use money; how willing or capable they are to take risks, and how they view their personal, business, or financial goals. By understanding clients' maps, you have a better basis for communicating with them.

Principle 1.3: *People develop preferential ways of processing information.* Over time, people build representational maps through accumulation of their life experiences. We use the five basic senses of seeing (visual), hearing (auditory), tasting (gustatory), smelling (olfactory), and feeling/action (kinesthetic) to acquire these experiences. Any one experience usually incorporates each of the five sensory elements. The same memory can be activated through any one of the five senses. While the smell of a bakery may activate images of home and childhood, the same memory may be activated by a particular taste, sound, or visual image. When we activate one sensory memory system, the others are automatically activated. Sensory-based representational maps provide the foundation for past, present, and future experiences and the basis for how we communicate about those experiences.

As people mature, they usually develop a preference for using one sensory system as a way of thinking about, or representing, the information they acquire. These preferences, often referred to as learning styles, include:

Auditory Learning: One person may prefer to learn and think about information he or she acquires through talking and listening.

Visual Learning: Another person may prefer to learn by watching others, seeing a film, or studying diagrams.

Kinesthetic Learning: A third person might prefer to learn through active participation. This type of learner usually uses trial and error or physical activity as a method of learning.

People very seldom develop only one learning style. Over time, and through formal education, individuals experience learning in all three ways. Usually, however, individuals develop preferences for one or more of the three styles. Knowledge of those three styles of learning can provide a basis for understanding how individuals differ and how communication occurs. For example, if a person learns best experientially, an auditory approach using lectures or discussions will probably be less effective than a method of communication that uses direct personal involvement. In this situation, some form of hands-on experience probably would facilitate communication.

Effective communication begins with knowledge you have about yourself and your clients. As a professional, you must be able to understand your client's representational map, and as we'll see, you must understand how this map is activated through your client's learning style. There are two aspects to this understanding:

▸You must assess your client's experiential, representational map as it relates to the purpose of your communication. In all professional relationships there are important issues, goals, or concerns. It is important for you to understand how your client views each so that you know what your client wants to achieve. For example, a financial planner needs to determine elements of a client's representational map about risk management, financial goals, diversification, or tax planning. A divorce lawyer needs to know a client's feelings about separation, divorce, communal assets, and custody.

▸It is important to know how your client prefers to process and represent information. If you have an awareness of how your client prefers to communicate, you will be able to alter your communicative patterns to engage your client in his or her preferred style. In essence, you will be able to enhance communication by speaking your client's language. This will enable clients to accept you and your ideas and will lead to effective communication.

Principle 1.4: *Changing information in one processing mode changes information in other processing modes*. The three learning styles refer to specific ways of processing information: visually, auditorily, and kinesthetically. As indicated in the discussion of Principle 1.3, most experiences incorporate elements of all senses. Therefore, when one sensory mode is activated, there is a tendency for each of the other sensory aspects of the experience to be activated as well. In professional communications, in our culture, the greatest concern is with auditory, visual, and kinesthetic processing. One form of kinesthetic processing refers to internal experiences: emotions, muscular, and glandular changes. The other form refers to external actions and activities. When we separate kinesthetic into internal and external experiences, we have an interactive system similar to Figure 1.

Figure 1

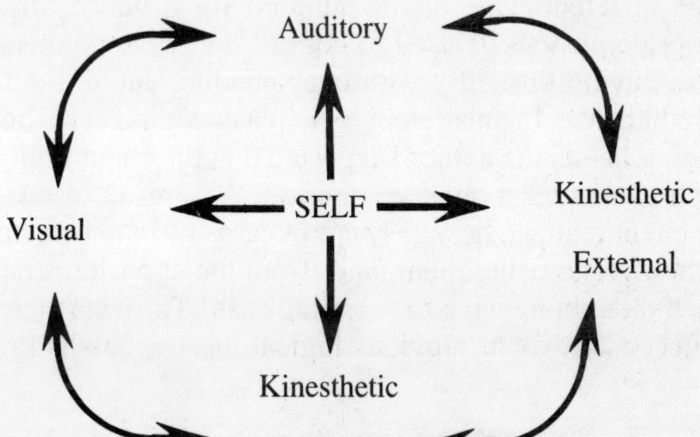

Notice how the arrows in the figure indicate the relationships among the processing modes. For example: visualize a lemon; then visualize cutting the lemon into quarters; visualize yourself holding the lemon close to your nose, and finally, visualize yourself biting into the juicy lemon. If you clearly visualize all this, you probably will become aware of an increase in saliva in your mouth and may feel your neck glands respond. The process of holding the images (visual) in your mind has an effect upon another processing mode (kinesthetic internal). This principle has a number of practical applications.

People can control their feelings, moods, and behavior by controlling what information they are processing. If you wish to relax, you can hold relaxing images in your mind and the body will relax accordingly.

This concept underlies several popular techniques taught to pregnant women to help them cope with labor pains. If you wish to change the way you think about a situation, but you find it difficult to do so, you can purposefully act in a manner opposite to the way you feel, which can actually affect your thoughts and feelings. When someone once asked Teddy Roosevelt how he could be so brave charging up San Juan Hill, Teddy responded, "I was really quite frightened, but if you act brave, then it can become true."

Helping people to achieve their goals or to change their behavior is accomplished more easily if we help them process appropriate information in one of the processing modes rather than by trying to *convince* them through logical argument that they should be different. One of the authors, for instance, discovered that this principle can be used to control unnecessary spending. A client was having difficulty with overspending due to the frequent use of credit cards. In an attempt to help a client to get in touch with his spending habits the author suggested that the client limit himself to cash purchases for a one-week period. As a result of this experience the client realized how easy credit cards were to use, how little thought he gave to using them, and, from the opposite perspective, how much thought he gave to spending cash! This short-term experience succeeded where previous logical discussions had failed.

Principle 1.5: *The number of choices people have at any point in time is directly related to the amount of detail in their representational maps*. This principle is best understood by example. Suppose you want to travel between two major cities in the same state. When you look at the average map from the local gas station, you will notice that the map contains only the major state and federal highways. In such situations, you usually will have only four or five different routes to choose from because there is limited detail on the map. If you were to obtain official county maps for all of the counties between the two cities, you would have enough detail to find every possible road between the two cities. With the additional maps and the additional detail, you would have a choice of many more possible routes. As the detail on the road map increases, the number of choices you have available to you increases. People's representational maps are similar. Freedom of choice increases with the amount of detailed information in a person's representational map.

The practical meaning of this principle in professional relationships is that as you increase the informational detail available to clients, you increase their freedom of choice. Increasing a client's freedom of choice builds trust, and the client will be less likely to feel roped into something.

There is, however, a possible danger with this principle. Sometimes there can be so much detail that choice becomes difficult or even impossible. At certain times people may believe they have information overload. For example, one of the authors watched a mother and father with a young son in a Baskin Robbins ice cream store. While they waited their turn to be served, the parents took turns picking the boy up and showing him all of the 31 flavors he had to choose from. Two things became very obvious. First, this was the boy's first trip to a Baskin Robbins. Second, the boy had no idea that there were so many ice cream choices in the world! As their number got closer and closer, the parents put more and more pressure on the boy to make his choice. The boy had never had so many choices in his life. He had too much detail. When their number was called for service, the boy, when asked what flavor he wanted, said, "I guess I'll just take chocolate." His parents then became somewhat irritated with the boy and said, "That's what you always have at home. Why do you think we brought you here?" The boy had so many choices he had become confused.

When people, like the boy at Baskin Robbins, get confused from too much detail, they usually fall back on what they know best. As you help clients add detail to their representational maps, you should monitor the amount of detail so that clients do not feel overloaded.

Principle 1.6: *People naturally generalize.* Each of us is continuously subjected to large quantities of information. To maintain sanity in a confusing environment, we learn to distinguish important messages from less important ones and, for efficiency, we learn to categorize sensory information into classes or subclasses. At a simple level, we soon learn that the burners on all stoves can be hot and that touching them can cause pain. We do not have to learn this lesson with each new stove that we encounter. We quickly form generalizations about stoves, burners, and physical pain.

In like manner, when you talk with clients, you soon become aware of generalizations they have created concerning the reason for your communication. For example, an insurance representative or financial planner may soon note that a particular client is against all life insurance because the individual previously had an unfavorable experience with an insurance agent. A physician may notice an unusual degree of mistrust in a patient who had several bad experiences with another doctor. In both of these examples the clients developed negative generalizations that can adversely affect the manner in which communication occurs with subsequent insurance representatives or physicians.

You, as a professional, also form generalizations. As you encounter clients, you classify them into categories around such variables as openness, resistance, cordiality, willingness, or risk-taking. You also form generalizations about the most appropriate ways of handling certain situations. As your professional experiences increase, your awareness of alternative actions increases. You form generalizations of concern, problems, and possible solutions. To a large degree, generalizations help you to be more effective and helpful to clients. The danger that often looms, however, is that you may grow to assume that your generalizations are true and then to act accordingly. There is little danger if your generalizations are positive. The real danger occurs when you form negative generalizations and then act upon them.

Remember, generalizations are hypotheses that we support from our experience. When we learn from experience that stove burners can be hot, we subsequently generalize and learn to be careful when testing stove burners. The generalization does not mean that all burners on all stoves are always hot, but it is a strong hypothesis. We learn to look carefully at burners, look to see if we can determine a recognizable color that would indicate heat, carefully place our hand over the burner to feel any possible heat, and, as a last resort, actually touch it. We are, in essence, testing our hypothesis. We must remember that our generalizations about people are also only strong hypotheses. We must test them in a manner similar to testing hot burners. If we remember that they are only hypotheses, we will be one step closer to developing effective communicative relationships.

Principle 1.7: *People process information differentially.* Recent research has indicated that the human brain is composed of two primary components, the left and right hemispheres, which have overlapping yet distinct functions. For most right-handed people, the left hemisphere of the brain specializes in logical-analytical thought and verbalization. Reading, writing, language, inference generation, theory building, and mathematics represent left hemispheric processes. The right hemisphere, by contrast, is primarily in control of spatial perception, perceptual insight, tactile sensation, and visualization. Intuitive, metaphoric, and inventive capacities; divergent thought; and some components of music and art ability are said to be functions of the brain's right hemisphere.

M.S. Gazzaniga, in his book *The Social Brain**, suggests that the brain has within it a number of *mental modules* that vary among individuals in number, location, and capacity. It is his belief that these modules express themselves through action (behavior) and not through verbal communication. Gazzaniga suggests that the brain's activities, the functions of both the left and right hemispheres and of the *mental modules*, are governed by a left hemispheric function he labels the *interpreter*.

In essence, the *interpreter* is responsible for integration of the individual's beliefs about the world *and* his or her actions in the world. Its task is to compare present action with previously held belief systems—conscious or subconscious. When a conflict occurs between belief and action, the *interpreter* attempts to reduce the conflict by one of two processes: changing the original belief or altering the conflicting behavior. For example, consider Bob, who for years has been telling everyone that when he can afford it, he is going to buy a particular make of automobile. Finally the time comes. Bob buys his wanted car. Let's say, to Bob's chagrin, that the new automobile turns out to be a real lemon—a dud—a zero! When Bob is asked how he likes the car he probably will say, "Oh, it's the greatest car I've ever owned!" Privately, however, Bob will

---

*All references are cited at the end of the book.

question his belief about this particular brand of automobile. He will be faced with the task of reducing the psychological gap created by his new knowledge and his previously held beliefs.

The ideas above apply to all of us. As people process information, they attempt to reduce "psychological gaps" through their left hemispheric *interpreter*. All humans operate, more or less, in a similar manner. Yet, each individual is also unique. Each person has a unique makeup. Males are different than females, right-handed people respond differently than those who are left-handed, and adolescents respond differently than adults. As communicators it is important to understand similarities and differences, to understand the importance of these differences in terms of communication, and to know how to assess differences.

Principle 1.8: *People seek informational harmony and closure*. As discussed in Principle 1.7, the interpreter module in the human brain seeks to organize behavior, beliefs, values, and needs in a consistent manner. The interpreter module does this by reducing psychological gaps. Whenever there is dissonance among any of our beliefs, values, or needs, there is motivation to reduce the dissonance and create *harmony*. This usually entails changing either a value or a belief so that they are consistent. For example, suppose a person has a basic need for security with his or her financial resources. This *belief* would usually lead that person to choose very conservative investment instruments such as FDIC insured bank notes. At the same time the person may place a high *value* on financial independence and learn from a financial planner that such a conservative investment will barely keep up with the inflation rate.

As a result of the new learning the person may develop a new *belief* that minimal risks must be taken if financial independence is to be achieved. However, this attitude may be in direct conflict with the individual's need for security. A person in such conflict will be motivated to change the need, value, or belief. Such a person may decide that financial security may not be as important as financial independence. Conversely, the person may decide that financial independence is not as important as financial security, and despite the information provided by the financial planner, stick to very secure, conservative investments. The latter decision could be reached even though the individual knows it may be contrary to "good" logic or "good" financial planning.

All of us have experienced times when we have an uneasiness or sense that something must be done. The feeling may be fear, nervousness, or frustration that results when we are forced to make choices relating to things that may be contrary to our beliefs, values, or needs. A third alternative always exists—we could avoid any action and not do anything, hoping that the situation will resolve itself. When we choose this alternative, we usually are left with the uneasy feeling of unresolved issues in our lives. When something in our lives activates the associated beliefs, values, or needs, emotions resulting from the unresolved issues can be triggered.

This need for informational harmony and the accompanying need to reduce dissonance among variables is probably central in most decision-making problems. As a financial professional, you must be aware of this and be patient. If you *press* a client when he or she is experiencing this sort of dissonance, expect resistance. Your persuasive efforts could be viewed as a high-pressure sales pitch. Dissonance cannot be resolved easily or quickly. Therefore, the best thing you can do is to allow the client time to resolve the dilemma and, when asked, to provide information that can aid the client in the decision-making process.

The second aspect of Principle 1.8 relates to the concept of *closure*. An example may be helpful in clarifying this concept. Suppose you are driving down the highway with a friend and you hear a song on the car radio. Your friend asks, "What's the name of that song?" You recognize the song as one that is very familiar to you. You have heard it a hundred times but, for the life of you, you can't remember the title. You may say something like, "Just a minute. It's on the tip of my tongue." You think for several seconds and can't remember it and then forget about it as you and your friend continue talking about other things. Later that evening, while you are doing something else, the title of the song pops into your head! What happened? Evidently, the human brain doesn't like to be left with unfinished business!

Below our level of awareness, at what is referred to as the subconscious level, work on problems continues until answers are found. There are a number of popular television commercials which incorporate this principle. One of the Budweiser beer commercials several years ago used the jingle, "When you say Budweiser, you've said it all!" At the end of the commercial you would hear the jingle again, but it ended after the word Budweiser,

"When you say Budweiser. . . ." Invariably, when people heard that phrase of the jingle, they would finish it in their heads. Even as you read the words now, there is the strong possibility that you have finished the jingle to yourself. This need to finish what has been started is the need for *closure*.

When people seek information and find closure, the information they find is likely to stay with them. In the example above, if you had attempted to remember the name of a song, you would be more likely to remember the title because of the work of your subconscious. In like manner, you would be more likely to remember Budweiser, when asked by a bartender for your choice of beer, if you had just heard the Budweiser jingle. It doesn't mean you will order a Budweiser, but it increases the likelihood that you will think of Budweiser when trying to decide which beer to order.

Principle 1.9: *People usually do what is best for themselves using stored information.* Each of us is dependent on information we have obtained and stored. As we move through life we gain new information, form new insights, and experience new situations. As new events occur, we respond to them from the perspective of our experiential map. We cannot do otherwise. "He's doing the best he can!" exemplifies this concept. An individual's actions will reflect stored information which, in some situations, may be incomplete or inaccurate.

The principle of closure has direct application in professional financial situations. One of the best times to apply this principle is when alternatives for action have been discussed but decisions for action have yet to be determined. For example, a financial professional might say to a client, "Now that we've discussed a number of possibilities it would be helpful if you gave some additional thought to the one you'd like to try. Think about the possibilities. Next week when we get together you can tell me about your decision. You might be surprised by what you come up with!"

The last sentence of the professional's statement would probably leave the client wondering what he or she might be surprised about. This is similar to the beer jingle in that the client would be left with a feeling of unfinished business. The approach used above allows the client an opportunity to consciously and subconsciously digest what has been discussed while allowing the natural process of closure to occur.

This principle suggests two areas important in professional relationships:

▸ First, you must help clients to assess information they have, help them to become aware of additional information important to their decision making, and help them to correct information that can be misleading.

▸ Second, you are obligated to continuously update your knowledge so that your professional interactions are based on the best possible information. Like your client, you are limited by the information you have. In the example from the prologue it is obvious the car salesperson either did not have up-to-date information about Fiero GT's or chose to ignore it. The quality of professional suggestion, advice, or counsel is dependent on continuously updated information.

There are two additional implications of the principle: First, sometimes simply correcting or adding new information may be enough to bring about dramatic changes in people's behavior. In most professional situations, such as sales or financial planning, the focus of the communicative interaction is on new information intended to motivate people in desired directions.

Second, although from our perspective people may be seen as engaging in self-defeating behavior, remember that, given the information they are using, they are doing the best they can. The best they can at any particular moment could be self-defeating. Additional information may be needed to affect their lives in a positive direction. This suggests the need for a positive attitude toward people and their behavior. It also implies that people aren't really resistant. They simply do the best they can given their stored information.

>>>**A TRAGIC EXAMPLE** → The most dramatic example of this principle is the person who attempts or commits suicide. For an outsider observing such behavior, it makes little sense that the individual chooses this act as an alternative to his or her problem. Yet, for the victim, with the information he has to work with, this may appear to be the best of bad choices. Remember, people do the best that they can with stored information, even though from the outside the choice may appear to be totally inappropriate.

Principle 1.10: *Communicative interactions are reciprocal.* When two people communicate, they do not talk at random. What one person says has an effect on the other. When the second person responds, it has an effect on the first and so on. There is mutual influence. When someone talks to you, you are affected in two ways.

▸ *The content of what is said limits the responses*. Usually only disturbed people will respond with a topic that has no relationship to what was said before. For example:

Psychiatrist: Well, how are you today, Mr. Fitzgerald?

Patient: What do you mean always barging in here and attacking me!

Psychiatrist: I just asked how you are today.

Patient: Oh, I know all about people like you. You just want to keep me here to take all my money.

▸ Second, *there is some emotional undertone to what people say* to you, usually expressed in their tone of voice, volume of their speech, and their nonverbal behavior. If the tone of voice, volume, and nonverbal behavior are consistent, we usually respond to the content in the same type of emotional undertone. When they are inconsistent, we are often confused, and either don't know how to respond, or we respond to the emotional undertone rather than to the content of what is said. For example:

Client (very loudly, while clenching his fist): I am not angry!

Professional (shouting back and looking very angry): ''You are too, and don't yell at me like that!''

Principle 1.9 indicates that people will usually influence the kinds of responses they receive from others. As our examples indicate, the reciprocal nature of communication can lead to a spiral in which one negative output generates a negative response, which in turn generates another negative output and so on. The same concept of reciprocity can produce positive communication spirals. Effective communication, of course, usually leads to positive spirals which are mutually beneficial.

A corollary concept is that we subconsciously form first impressions and expectations of how our communicative interaction will proceed. When the response we get from another person does not meet those expectations or fit our initial impressions, either we are initially confused or we tend to respond to the nonverbal message, such as the look on the person's face or his or her gestures. Verbal messages typically used by parents exemplify this. For example:

Parent: Don't look at me in that tone of voice!

or

Parent: Wipe that silly grin off your face!

These familiar phrases are the parent's response to our nonverbal behavior rather than to our words.

> ⋙**BE CONSISTENT**→ The old adage "Actions speak louder than words" also exemplifies this concept. Effective communicators respond to people within their expectations and respond with both nonverbal and verbal consistency.

Principle 1.11: *The majority of stored information/learning is not conscious.* Humans seem to equate learning and knowledge with what they *know* at any point in time. What individuals *know* at any point in time is what they are *conscious* of. Yet, this conscious knowledge is a very small portion of total knowledge. The world we are aware of includes both the environment around us and the thoughts that are constantly active in our minds. Thus, while writing, an author is aware of the computer keyboard, the monitor, the television playing in the background, and the notes on the typing stand. These are all in the "environment" outside. If attention is focused more broadly, the author can become aware of the chair he is sitting on, his feet on the floor, and so on. While typing, he is aware of the various thoughts that come to mind as he is trying to express his ideas. This is quite a bit to be aware of at one time. This is what he is *conscious* of while he is typing. He is not aware of, or does not have in his consciousness, all of the things that happened at work during the day. He is not aware of memories about last week or memories of things that happened when he was a child or a teenager.

Although much of the stored information is below his level of consciousness, it is the basis for his behavior even though he is not conscious of it at the moment. For example, he spent many months practicing and learning how to type. It was a frustrating time and took a great deal of time and effort. The process of learning to type was a slow process of identifying a key, finding it on the keyboard, placing the correct finger over it, and pressing. Each letter had to be *consciously* found and *consciously* pressed. With each practice session, the finding of keys became more automatic, or subconsciously controlled. With enough practice, a good typist doesn't think about letters or keys. The good typist just thinks words, and the fingers seem to respond with their own will to produce the word on the keyboard. In a real sense the process of typing becomes a subconscious process. A great deal of our behavior, feelings, values, and beliefs are of the same nature. Once they are learned, they seem to operate *automatically* or *subconsciously*.

A second concept underlying this principle is that very often a person's explanations for his or her behavior may represent only a portion of information that was used to generate the behavior. Previously, we discussed the operation of a mental element called the *interpreter*. The interpreter attempts to explain our behavior in a congruent and socially acceptable manner. When it does, the person may be *conscious* of only part of the information that formed the basis of the behavior. The socially acceptable explanation may represent only part of the information. This does not mean that people deliberately lie to you or to themselves. It does mean that, very often, the conscious information used to explain one's behavior is only part of a fuller explanation. It is this deeper and fuller understanding of the information people use to generate behavior which is the target of most counseling or therapy processes. We do not mean to imply that you must become a therapist to become an effective communicator. We do mean to say that effective communicators are always aware that there are fuller explanations for an individual's behavior than even the person understands. Keeping this principle in mind can allow you to flow with the inconsistencies in client communication that may, on the surface, sound like little white lies.

CHAPTER 2

The Communication Process

This chapter presents eight conceptual communication principles that provide the basis for understanding the process of communication. Everything a person does communicates something, even doing nothing. People communicate through a variety of modes: words, nonverbal behavior, use of space, and variations in voice tonality, volume, and speed. There are important differences between the ways males and females communicate, differences which can have a major impact on professional relationships. There are a number of influences on and obstacles to effective communication. The principles to be discussed in this chapter are:

> ***Principle 2.1:*** An individual cannot NOT communicate.
> ***Principle 2.2:*** People use words, actions, space, and tonality, rate, and volume to communicate.
> ***Principle 2.3:*** Males and females develop different communicative styles.
> ***Principle 2.4:*** Initial impressions affect communicative interactions.
> ***Principle 2.5:*** When a person's world is stopped, he or she pays full attention.
> ***Principle 2.6:*** Communication has five major components and two process elements.
> ***Principle 2.7:*** Communication is constantly being influenced.
> ***Principle 2.8:*** Communication always has its obstacles.

Consider the following: George was interested in helping his youngest daughter to obtain information about trade schools. George identified an educational consultant, one he knew on a casual basis; called him; told him of his needs; and scheduled an appointment. To George's disbelief, his consultant "friend" said, "George, don't worry about that nonsense. Your daughter will do fine without your help!" George overcame his initial shock and again asked for an appointment. A date was set for late Friday afternoon the following week. George prepared himself for the meeting by carefully examining his information needs, collecting what he thought were relevant materials, and preparing himself mentally for the discussion. George entered the meeting with high hopes and a great deal of curiosity. To George's chagrin, the consultant was late for the meeting (in his own office!), came dressed in shorts and a T-shirt, didn't appear to be prepared for the meeting, and, in general, acted in an unprofessional manner. George left the meeting confused and frustrated.

Principle 2.1: *People cannot NOT communicate.* Everything an individual does communicates something. What is communicated may not be what was intended, but communication does occur nonetheless. Consider a person who, when confronted with a new situation, becomes withdrawn and very silent. Is this individual *not* communicating, or could the person be communicating that he or she is shy, uneasy, and unsure? You might think that you really don't know what the person is thinking or feeling. This is probably true. Yet, you will, and do, form opinions about individuals like the one mentioned.

These opinions are formed from your observations of the person, and your subsequent thoughts and actions will be triggered by your opinions. In a true sense you have been affected by the other person. He or she communicated *something* about his or her inner world, and this something has affected you.

Let's apply this principle to our friend George and his encounter with the inexperienced educational consultant. George's reaction to the encounter would probably be (1) that the consultant did not care enough to prepare himself for his interview, (2) that George was relatively unimportant, and (3) that George's fears or worries were unfounded. On what basis might George form these opinions? Principle 2.2 provides an answer.

Principle 2.2: *People use words, actions, space, tonality, rate, and volume to communicate.* Communication occurs in many ways. Some of these ways are more obvious than others. Edward T. Hall, in a classic text, *The Silent Language,* documented a number of channels people use for communication. We will consider four of those channels.

Verbal Channel: Words. The verbal channel is the one with which we are most familiar. The words we speak and the concepts we express through language are the primary focus of most of our communicative behavior. But, as we discussed in Chapter 1, words do not have the same meaning for everyone. For example, *risk-taking* to one person may mean making a five-dollar wager on a sporting event, while to another person it may mean borrowing a substantial amount of money to make an investment. We depend on the verbal channel for communication. Yet, we must keep in mind that the words people use are only the tip of the iceberg. Words provide us *some* information, but by no means *all* of what we must know to understand another's experiential map of the world.

George's words expressed a desire to provide for his daughter's well-being. His consultant's words suggested that George shouldn't worry. In both cases the *words* provided a portion of the entire message, but not all that transpired between the two men.

Nonverbal Channel. The second channel is nonverbal. The old saying "A picture is worth a thousand words" is also appropriate in interpersonal communications. In fact, some experts say that up to 90% of all communication is nonverbal. As an example of this, remember when, as a child, a look from one of your parents would freeze you with fear. Nonverbally, your parents communicated to you loudly and clearly. Most parents intuitively learn to use the power of nonverbal communication. Skilled communicators, like skilled parents, use this channel easily and purposefully. Professionals can become more powerful in their interactions and more skilled in communications by paying attention to their own nonverbal communication and to that of their clients.

Once more, let's review George and his interaction. It is clear that George cared about his meeting. He came prepared with questions. He was on time. He was seeking solutions to his concerns. On the other hand, the consultant was late for the meeting. He was dressed in sports attire, and he was casual in posture and actions. In this interaction the *nonverbal behavior* speaks louder than the *verbal*.

Space. The third channel, space, can be a powerful form of communication. For instance, an experience we've all had demonstrates the power of spatial communication. Consider friends or acquaintances who meet on the street, stop to say hello, and catch up on old news. Frequently, when they are about to part they say something like "Let's get together sometime for lunch." This statement is usually made as both people are backing away from each other. A typical "Yeah, let's do that sometime . . ." concludes the conversation. In this situation both parties are implying "Let's get together; it's fun to talk." However, the increasing space, as they talk, communicates distance and separateness. Usually, the space speaks more loudly and with more authority than the words. The individuals probably will not get together for lunch.

Other examples of space (and how it is used in communication) can be drawn from our daily lives and how we have been conditioned to use personal space. Hall refers to *dimensions* of space. His findings provide us an interesting description of how we use space to communicate. He suggests that people, as a result of cultural influences, abide by unwritten yet clearly defined rules of space. Here is typical American practice:

▸ We normally keep people we don't know at least 36 inches away. This is considered to be *public* space.

▸ We allow individuals we know, but not well, a little closer, approximately 30-36 inches. This is called *social* space.

▸ Individuals whom we know and trust we will allow to get as close as 24 inches from us. This is called *personal* space.

▸ For us to allow individuals closer than 24 inches we must be very comfortable with them and usually know them extremely well. This distance, 0-24 inches is called *intimate* space.

All of these space distances are averages and are subject to sexual, religious, and subcultural variances. Nonetheless, they provide a basis for understanding communication and a means for influencing the communicative process. For example, a simple pat on the back intended as a gesture of friendliness on the part of a professional may make a client uncomfortable. If both the client and the financial professional are men, the client may think the financial professional is being too friendly. If the client is female and the financial professional male, a pat on the back may be experienced as too intimate. Another example is when the financial professional, wishing to emphasize a point, leans forward to talk intently to a client, who may experience pressure to choose a particular investment. Effective communicators are aware of how their use of space affects others, and consequently they use it to make others feel comfortable.

How was the concept of space used in George's situation? If you recall, George and the consultant were separated by the consultant's desk. This physical barrier can be a psychological barrier and can interfere with the communication process. Consequently, as an effective communicator you should be aware of the power of space and use it to enhance relationships and not to impede them. (For more on effective use of space, see Chapter 8.

Tonality, Rate, and Volume. Yet another channel we use for communication is our voice and the limitless combinations of tonality, speech rate, and volume we can create. It is usually relatively easy to tell whether someone is angry or depressed by his or her tone of voice, speech volume, and speech rate. Angry people tend to talk loudly, have an edge to their voices, and speak much faster than normal. Sad people tend to talk in a very flat tone, speak with lower volume, and speak much slower than normal. While these two extremes are relatively easy to identify, there are many gradations between the two.

Communication can be enhanced by paying attention to the subtle differences you detect. There are times when people are unaware of how they use tonality, rate, and volume to express aspects of their experience. It often happens between spouses. One spouse will say something in a loud, angry voice, such as "why didn't you enter the last two checks you wrote?" The other spouse might reply, "Don't yell at me!"—to which the first spouse responds with a shout, "I'm not yelling!" In this familiar situation, the second spouse didn't respond to the words of the first spouse as much as to the tone and volume of what was said. The first spouse's response indicates that there was little or no awareness of the tone and volume of the initial communication.

This kind of situation raises an interesting question. Which is more important to respond to: the words or the tone, rate, and volume? In general, effective communicators respond to both. They respond to the words in such a way that they communicate understanding and, also, recognize the second message communicated through tone, rate, and volume. Using our spouse example once again, an effective communicator might reply, "You sound angry at me for not recording the checks." Effective communicators learn to recognize all of the channels of communication and to respond to them appropriately.

There is another issue related to the difference that exists between words and tone, rate, and volume. There are situations in which a person's words communicate one meaning and tone, rate, and volume communicate something entirely different. For example, a person might say in a low, flat tone of voice and very slowly, "I'm so happy." When we hear such a statement, we intuitively know that something is wrong. Happy people usually don't speak in those tones. The tone, rate, and volume are inconsistent with the words. Often, when people speak to us that way, they themselves aren't aware of the inconsistency. What are we to respond to: the words or tone, rate, or volume? What usually is occurring in such a situation is that people are happy at a conscious level; and secondly that they are sad, depressed, or feeling low at a subconscious level. There is the tendency to automatically respond to the second message as if it were the more important. Effective communicators usually respond to both messages by labelling each half of the communication. The response could be "You say you're happy, but you sound sad," or "While you say you're happy, your voice sounds depressed." Effective communicators do not assume that one message is more important than the other.

Nonverbal behavior, space, tonality, rate, and volume provide subtle cues to another person's map of the world. It is important that we notice these cues so that we form meaningful hypotheses about what they might mean. In the movie *10,* the hero, played by Dudley Moore, is enthralled by the heroine, played by Bo Derek. He observes her from afar and creates, in his mind, a picture of who she is and how she would act. Yet, when he pursues a relationship with her, he finds her to be quite different than anticipated. In fact, she is so different that he is shocked!

Many of us, like the hero of *10*, observe individuals, form an impression, and only later realize that our impression was inaccurate. We respond to the many individual nuances of the person and compare our observations of this person with persons we have known in the past. If we see a high degree of similarity between the new acquaintance and others we have known, we assume that the new person is *like* the others we have known. At a subconscious level, we depend on our interpersonal observations and history with others to provide a basis for all of our interpersonal interactions.

Principle 2.3: *Males and females develop different communicative styles.* Judy Cornelia Pearson (1985) provides considerable insight into differences in male and female communicative styles. Our goal is to present those differences that appear to be most important to professional relationships.

Differences in communication between the sexes can be found in all channels of communication. In the verbal channel, for instance, there are a number of differences between how males and females communicate. The first significant difference is in the formality of language. Females tend to use formal words and phrases, whereas males are more likely to use informal ones. For instance, a female might say, "I understand what you are trying to tell me," while, by contrast, a male might say, "I get the picture." Females appear to *prefer* the specificity that language can provide, while males appear to focus on underlying principles or issues. When financial professionals work with couples, they should be aware of this typical difference between males and females. They should adjust their speech so that both approaches will be accommodated—the search for specificity and the tendency to conceptualize. One approach is neither better or worse than the other, they are merely different. And the difference can often lead to misunderstanding and conflict.

Males often feel they are explaining a concept and find that females responding to their statements focus on the accuracy of the words being used rather than on the ideas being relayed. Males then may judge that the females do not understand or are being unnecessarily picky about the choice of words. For example, assume that a financial professional says the following: "When we consider real estate limited partnerships as a tax shelter there is always the question of risk. We have to consider the risk relative to the potential losses. Suppose we consider taxes paid as *lost*. If the limited partnership investment reduces your taxes 80% for the length of the partnership, and if it does fold, you have *lost* the amount you invested less the amount saved in your taxes." According to Pearson's work, a female might respond, "I'm confused. What do you mean lost? I thought I was investing money. How can investing in a losing proposition be the same as paying taxes?" As stated, females tend to pay attention to specifics. In the same situation a male might respond, "I see. Since taxes are lost it doesn't make any difference if I lose money to the government or in the investment."

Misunderstanding often occurs when people use examples to illustrate a point. A male may think the example helps to clarify the concept only to find that the female takes exception with the example or the words used rather than focusing on the principle or concept he was attempting to communicate.

A second major difference can be found in the *nature* of the words or phrases used. Males and females differ in their tendencies to use hostile words, profanity, or expletives. Males are considerably more likely to lace their conversation with words of this type than are females. In general, men tend to have a much more earthy quality to their language. Females, by contrast, use more precise descriptions and are less likely to reveal overt aggressiveness in their speech.

A third difference exists. According to Pearson, males are less likely to use hyper correction, intensifiers, fillers, qualifiers, or disclaimers than females. Let's look at each of these. Hyper correction is excessively correcting what another person said. Females tend to respond with precision to the meaning of words. Males, on the other hand, seem to be content with the overall meaning being conveyed. Given this difference, it seems to be more important for females to respond to the exact meaning of the spoken word and for males to react to the totality of the communication. For females, hyper correction may be a means of evaluating whether they have understood the speaker's message. Males, apparently, are content with understanding the overall message and are less concerned about how the message is given.

Intensifiers like "so," "quite," and "awfully" illustrate the second category in this general type. Females are more likely to say something like "This is an awfully big challenge" or "That is a great deal more than I had hoped for." Males would probably say "This is a challenge" or "That's more than I had hoped for." Females, in general, use intensifiers to increase the importance of what is being stated.

Both sexes use fillers, but females use them more frequently, especially as feedback. Fillers like "um hmm," "okay," and "right" are vocalized utterances that are used to assure the speaker that they are being attended to or understood. Males are more likely to provide such feedback to the speaker in a nonverbal manner, perhaps through direct eye contact or through nonverbal behavior such as a head nod.

Qualifiers like "maybe," "in my opinion," "perhaps," "somewhat," and "in general" are used not only to generalize specific statements but also to soften the impact of what has been communicated. If you look back through this discussion you will see a number of "qualifiers." These have been used to suggest that "in many cases but not exclusively" males and females respond differently. Females use this form of communication more frequently than males do.

In addition, disclaimers are found in females' speech more often than in males' speech. The following are examples of disclaimers: "I know I don't know much about this, but __," or "I probably will get in your way, but, __ " or "If you don't mind, could you __?" In all of these examples the disclaimer sets the listener up for some plea or request and consequently can lead to confusion.

Principle 2.4: *Initial impressions affect communicative interactions.* In a book titled *Contact,* Zunin and Zunin state that the first four minutes of an interpersonal interaction are "the key to establishing social relationships, family harmony, business success, and sexual pleasure." This first four minutes is the average time span in which people assess each other and arrive at decisions of whether to pursue or to terminate the relationship. Given the significance of these first minutes, one might ask, "What, specifically, are people responding to?" The following elements appear to be most important.

Trustworthiness. An individual will trust another initially if certain criteria are met. The first reaction is visually based. When you meet people for the first time, you subconsciously assess what they are wearing, how they stand or sit, how they posture themselves, how they move, and how they use nonverbal gestures in communication. You pay particular attention to eye contact, the manner in which they say or form words, the sound of the voice, and the speed of their speech. You use each of these bits of data to arrive at your overall assessment, usually at a subconscious level. (In Chapter 5 we discuss how you can use specific behaviors to enhance trustworthiness in these first few minutes.)

At a more conscious level, you also attend to what is said. If you determine that the person does understand the important issues under discussion, then you probably will be more favorably disposed toward him or her. Your overall rating of trustworthiness is dependent upon your reactions to all of these variables.

Societal Expectations. We have all met people we immediately like. By contrast, we have met people who turn us off! What is the difference? Probably some combination of the factors outlined above. For example, imagine yourself going to a meeting in which you are introduced to a forty-year-old man. He is clean-shaven and is wearing a well-tailored, navy blue pinstriped suit. He carries himself in an athletic manner, has a ready smile, and appears to be interested in what you have to say. He looks at you when you talk. He nods his head in understanding. Overall, he demonstrates good listening skills. Most people would immediately like such a person. The person described fits a number of normal societal expectations. In general, the more we fit societal and subgroup expectations of success, the more likely we will be accepted by others. In this regard, being viewed as different is a disadvantage. To avoid being viewed as different, we must become aware of what is expected and learn to act accordingly.

Dynamic Quality. A person who demonstrates a sense of excitement for living, a forceful presence, an enthusiasm for interpersonal involvements, and a willingness to entertain new ideas or behaviors usually will be viewed in a positive manner by others. People who demonstrate these characteristics in initial encounters will attract others to them.

Basic Value Similarity. In initial interactions, people attempt to determine the basic values of others. The degree to which another is openminded, the degree to which an individual is impartial or unbiased, and the degree to which another expresses views similar to one's own—all are determined very early in a relationship. If you determine that another is similar to you, then a basic sense of trust and liking probably will follow.

Status. In addition to the above, there are status determinants of trust and liking. In this regard, people of higher status command, and receive, communicative responses that reflect their status position. For example, the manager of a credit union, by the nature of his or her position, will be given greater credibility than an employee of the credit union by those people who are aware of the status of both persons. As unfair as it may seem, position or status carries power or influence. The higher the status, the greater the power.

Principle 2.5: *When a person's world is stopped, he or she pays full attention.* This principle may seem more abstract than those already presented. Yet, an understanding of this principle can facilitate communication. Underlying this principle is the orienting reflex common to all animals. The orienting reflex simply means that when something different happens in the environment we will pay attention to it long enough to decide whether it is potentially dangerous. We normally pay attention to only a limited amount of stimuli that bombard us at any point in time. We habituate, or adjust, to any stimuli that aren't included in our immediate focus of attention. When some stimulus in the environment is different than normal expectations, we usually stop to pay attention to it.

For example, while you are watching television you gradually pay less and less attention to the normal noise of the children playing in the house. You habituate to the playing noises and pay attention to the television. However, when one of the children screams, you suddenly pay attention. You focus on the scream to see if it indicates that it is just part of normal play or whether it means someone is hurt. If you decide it is part of normal play, you focus your attention back on the television. If you decide it may mean someone is hurt, you will rush to see what happened. When the orienting reflex is activated, you give your full attention for a moment. By full attention we mean that all of your senses are focused on the stimulus until you decide, consciously or subconsciously, how you need to respond.

In a general way, we are aware that unusual occurrences cause us to stop and to reassess our world, such as the teenager who has a close friend die in a car accident, the man who has his youngest child leave home, the woman who loses a job, or the people who observe a televised space shuttle explosion. In all of these situations, individuals are forced to reconsider what they believe to be important in life.

Even though the nature of most intervening events may not be as dramatic as those presented above, effective communicators can use this human capacity for attending to important circumstances to help their clients. A realtor working in a small town in New York had a client who was interested in purchasing a tract of land outside of town for building a residence. As a result of a number of conversations, she learned that the client frequently sought out such property, but never purchased. In the course of discussing potential sites, the realtor said, "I'm aware that you have looked at property in the past and that you look but don't buy. Could it be that you are afraid to take the risk?" This question caught the client off guard and led to an in-depth discussion that focused on all the positives and negatives about living outside the town limits. The realtor, in this situation, had gone beyond the words of the client and had addressed an apparently deeper concern. To get at this concern, the realtor had to confront the client with his own behavior. The realtor's statement stopped the client's usual means of operating, and that led to greater understanding for both.

A second way to look at this principle is to consider the concept of psychological patterns. Patterns are generalizations that make it easier to function in a stimulus-loaded environment. We have learned, for instance, that when we see a police officer, we should behave lawfully; that when we see a school bus, we should drive cautiously; or that when we are at public events and the National Anthem is played, we should stand and place our hand over our heart. Each of these learnings becomes a pattern that no longer requires conscious thought. Each helps us to function in society. There are patterns, however, that interfere with our functioning. In the example presented above, the realtor became aware of her client's pattern and, through making an unexpected comment, helped the client examine how that pattern influenced his decisions. By helping a person recognize a pattern, a financial professional can help an individual *stop his or her world* and gain control over an otherwise subconscious occurrence.

Principle 2.6: *Communication has five major components and two process elements.* Communication is a complex act in which two or more people attempt to share internal thoughts and feelings. In the process of this sharing, a number of variables affect the nature and content of communication. The major components of this process are the *sender,* the *message,* the *channel,* the *receiver,* and the *environment.* The process elements inherent in this act are *feedback* and *noise.*

▸ The *sender* is the originator of the message. In human interaction, the sender is the person who wishes to convey a thought or feeling. An insurance salesperson who expresses an opinion about a specific policy to a client is a sender, a client who mentions to a CPA that he wants to shelter more income is a sender, and a financial professional who explains the use of options to a client is a sender.

▸ The *message* is the idea or feeling that is conveyed by the sender. The message for the insurance salesperson mentioned above might be that the policy under discussion can meet the client's specific needs. For the client working with the CPA the message might be "I want help." For the financial professional, the message might be "These are the implications of options that I would like you to understand." In each case, the message serves as the content being transmitted.

▸Communicative messages are sent through *channels.* In the human system the five senses of sight, sound, touch, taste, and smell are the channels through which messages are exchanged. Of these, sight and sound are the most important. Hamilton, Parker, and Smith suggest that language, paralanguage, and nonverbal language are the three primary channels of communication. They also suggest that the spoken word accounts for 7% of communication, that 38% of communication is through paralanguage (voice intonation, rhythm, inflection, etc.), and that nonverbal language (gestures, use of space, body movements, etc.) is responsible for the remaining 55% of what is communicated. It is noteworthy that they ascribe 100% of communication to channels involving sight and sound and totally disregard taste or smell as channels of communication. They do, however, consider touch as an important variable in nonverbal language. (Remember, they are talking about the process of channelling communication. People do store information with elements of *all* the senses.) Finally, sight and sound are emphasized because of cultural expectations. In our culture sight and sound are the primary channels. In other cultures or subcultures, smell and taste may be very important communication channels.

The three channels of sight, sound, and touch are primarily responsible for the degree to which an intended message is communicated. For example, if a client said to a lawyer, "I'm very happy to be working with you," while he looked and acted disinterested, a dual message could be communicated. On the one hand, the client might be saying "I'm happy to be working with you." On the other hand, the client, through paralanguage and nonverbal language, appears to be saying "I'm not happy to be working with you." For accurate communication, it is important that the individual sending the message, the *sender,* be consistent across channels. That is, it is important that the same message be sent across all of the channels of communication. This will assure that the message is transmitted with the greatest clarity. It is the sender's responsibility to assure that the message that is intended is communicated in a consistent manner.

▸The *receiver* is recipient of the message, the person, to whom the message is directed, and as such has an obvious influence on whether communication will occur. In this capacity the *receiver* must demonstrate openness to the incoming message and capability for responding.

▸The receiver uses *feedback,* the first of the process elements, to carry out his or her responsibility. Feedback is the response or reaction the receiver provides the sender about the message and how it was communicated. As a result of the receiver's feedback, the client would have an opportunity to correct or alter his or her message. The lawyer in the example above might provide feedback to the client by saying, "I'm confused. You say that you are happy to be working with me, but you don't seem happy." This allows the client to clarify which message is most important, the verbal or the nonverbal.

▸The *environment* is the context in which communication takes place. Obviously, it is difficult to hold another's attention in a hot, humid, or poorly ventilated room. The receiver's ability to attend is directly related to the degree of his or her physical comfort. Therefore, it is very important for financial professionals to provide a physical environment that is conducive to attentiveness and understanding.

The second environmental variable that must be considered is psychological in nature. Environments, by their very nature, will be comfortable or uncomfortable. For example, a student in a principal's office will be less comfortable than the principal. A banker in her office will be more comfortable than a customer seeking a loan. From a practical, applied point of view, a financial professional must consider the psychological environment and do whatever is necessary to ensure that the receiver (the client) is psychologically comfortable. In some circumstances, this may mean holding conferences in the client's environment or in a neutral arena.

▸Noise can be either internal or external in nature. Internal noise occurs in communication when either participant has a physical or psychological malady; if either party is preoccupied with other thoughts; or, in general, when one or both of the people involved have difficulty focusing on the message. External noise is usually easier to detect and, frequently, easier to remedy. External noise consists of variables such as heat, sounds, humidity, odors, ventilation, and so on. Each of these can influence the attentiveness of the receiver and the communicative impact of the sender. It is the financial professional's responsibility to be aware of the influence of environment on communications and to create a physical environment that is conducive to attentiveness and understanding.

Principle 2.7: *Communication is constantly being influenced.* There are many influences on the communicative process.

Motivation is a key influence in interaction that refers to the internal state of both the sender and receiver. If either party is not motivated to communicate, then the degree to which both parties understand the primary meaning of messages will be decreased. For instance, if an accountant is attempting to help her client to understand the necessities of obtaining tax-sheltered investments, while the client is thinking about an upcoming golf outing, then meaningful message transfer probably is not taking place. What could cause such a situation? Many things! The client could be overworked, the room might be too hot, or the financial need, at the moment, may not be sufficiently pressing to the client. The important point is that for true communication to occur, both parties have to be motivated. In professional relationships, it is the professional's responsibility to promote motivated interaction and to be aware when this is not occurring. One of the purposes of this book is to show you ways to accomplish this end. Subsequent chapters will present skills designed for making communication more effective.

Source credibility is a second issue to be considered. If we believe someone is important, we are more likely to listen to him or her. If we accept this basic assumption, then it becomes crucial for us to be viewed by our clients as being important. A professional obtains credibility in many ways—by demonstrating excellence with past clients; by behaving in a professionally competent manner with current clients; by establishing a reputation for excellence in the professional field; and by being professionally visible through books, articles, and speeches. Source credibility is important, yet fragile. It is difficult to achieve and relatively easy to lose. A credible professional must continuously work to stay abreast of current developments in his or her field and must demonstrate credibility in interactions with clients. In essence, credibility occurs when professionals have a substantial knowledge base, stay current with their field, and demonstrate their knowledge through a caring interaction.

Information difficulty is an important variable to consider. If we assume that the professional is motivated and able to motivate the client and further that the professional has a high degree of credibility, then we probably would assume that clients would be willing to expend effort to learn what is necessary for making meaningful changes in their lives. This assumption will hold if the information clients are asked to learn or deal with is not overly difficult. For many clients, the difficulty level of communicated information determines whether they pay attention to the professional's message. Information that is too difficult will not be attended to or will not be accepted in a manner that is beneficial. This is true for both written and verbal communication.

Organization has a significant impact on the degree to which information is learned. Two basic principles can be applied to organization.

▸ The first, the principle of *primacy,* suggests that information that occurs early in an interchange is likely to be remembered longer and in greater detail than material that occurs in the middle of the interchange.

▸ The second principle, the principle of *recency,* suggests that the last information presented will be remembered with clarity.

Although which of these two principles is dominant isn't specified, it is clear that information occurring early (primacy) and information occurring late (recency) are more likely to be remembered than materials presented in the middle of an interchange.

A professional can utilize these principles by organizing materials in such a way that the most important elements of a message occur early and/or late in the interaction. For example, a doctor, in consultation with a patient, could use these principles by saying the following: "It is important that you consume more fluids than normal. One of the problems that you are presently experiencing is related to your diet, the amount of exercise that you are getting, and the way that your body is processing what you have been ingesting. This problem is quite common and not very serious, but I would suggest that you consume more fluids than you normally do." Notice that the doctor's primary message about increasing fluids is given both early and late in his statement.

Communicative style is the final influence on communication to be discussed in this section. Although style can be viewed from many perspectives, we will be concentrating on one that emphasizes interaction. *Style* refers to how you, as a professional, represent yourself to the client. We will present three possibilities, even though, by forming combinations of the three, many others exist.

▸ As a professional you can approach the client from an authority/expert perspective. From this stance, communication focuses on what *you know* and how the client can benefit from your knowledge. Information is emphasized. Decisions are reached from logical analysis of known data. Although you can be cordial in the interchange, the communicative atmosphere is structured. You determine what will be discussed and how decisions should be reached. A brief example of this approach might look like the following:

Professional: The best investment possibility open to you is a limited partnership. This will provide you all of the tax sheltering you need and give a fair cash flow advantage.

Client: Why is this the best for me?

Professional: Your tax bracket makes it imperative that you shelter some of your income. Also, this vehicle has the best combination of shelter and income. You will benefit more from this investment than from any of the others I've described to you.

▸ A professional could also adopt a communicative style that would emphasize facilitation. In this approach, you provide relevant information but emphasize the *client's understanding* and use of the information. You can use communicative skills to help the client to arrive at personally relevant decisions. In contrast to the authority/expert approach, this approach or style places greater responsibility on the client. An interchange using this approach might flow like the following:

Professional: We've examined a number of investment possibilities. Which one looks best to you?

Client: From what we've discussed I'm leaning toward a limited partnership.

Professional: What is it about limited partnerships that you find attractive?

▸ Finally, a professional could adopt a communicative style that is *low key* or laissez faire in nature. In this approach you place almost all of the responsibility on the client and provide information specifically sought by the client. This approach is reactive instead of proactive. Again, an example might clarify this style:

Professional: What are your needs?

Client: I'd like to examine some investment possibilities.

Professional: Which ones have you considered?

Client: Well, I've looked at a number of them.

Professional: Have you settled on any in particular?

Client: Limited partnerships look quite good. What can you tell me about them?

It should be obvious that the examples presented above are stereotypical. Yet, they do reflect a variety of communicative styles open to professionals. The choice of any one style, or combination of styles, is dependent on client needs, professional competency, personality variables of the professional and his or her clients, the context in which the communication is occurring, and the nature of the professional endeavor.

Principle 2.8: *Communication always has its obstacles.* Communication, by its very nature, is less than perfect. The message transmitted from sender to receiver will always be less than 100%. As a professional, your goal should be to maximize the receiver's understanding of the message. To do this, awareness of a number of obstacles can help you communicate more effectively.

Inadequate preparation is one of the potential obstacles. A realtor who doesn't know current mortgage rates, a doctor who doesn't know current practices, a financial professional who doesn't know current investment vehicles, or an insurance salesperson who doesn't know insurance benefits will communicate with their clients, but not what they might want to communicate. Remember, effective communication is based on credibility. As discussed earlier, credibility results when knowledge is demonstrated. Inadequate preparation prevents you from displaying this knowledge and destroys credibility. The end result can be the client's lack of faith in you, a subsequent lack of motivation in the communicative process, and eventually, a severing of the professional relationship. Without this relationship, there is no communication!

Vague instructions can also interfere with the communicative process. Clients frequently are unaware of the subtle aspects of professional discussions. Consequently, vague statements, unclear instructions, inexact definitions, or obscure procedures can lead to client confusion. It is important for you to be as clear and succinct as possible so that interferences to communication are prevented.

Failure to follow rules is a general catchall category. There are a number of rules, which, when neglected, prevent facilitative communication.

▸*Rule one.* You should attempt to provide an overall perspective about the topic under discussion. Communication is enhanced when clients know how specific pieces of data fit into the overall picture.

▸*Rule two.* You should use the simplest words possible to get your message across. A minimum of simple, succinct words is far superior to many confusing terms.

▸*Rule three.* Be specific. A client should know what, exactly, is being discussed. You should try to avoid generalities and to be pointed in the messages you communicate.

▸*Rule four.* Use repetition in your communication. Clients are more likely to *hear* messages that are repeated a number of times. This rule becomes especially important when it is coupled with the principles of *primacy* and *recency*.

CHAPTER 3

The Professional Relationship

Effective professional relationships do not just happen; they follow important principles and develop through orderly stages which can be identified and promoted through the use of appropriate skills. The principles to be discussed in this chapter are as follows:

> ***Principle 3.1:*** The purpose of professional relationships is to influence and motivate.
>
> ***Principle 3.2:*** Six dimensions exist in an ideal professional relationship: openness, realistic expectations, structure, power, confirmation of differences, and mutual involvement.
>
> ***Principle 3.3:*** Professional relationships progress through four stages: initiating, exploring, understanding, and acting.
>
> ***Principle 3.4:*** Specific professional relationships have specific developmental stages.
>
> ***Principle 3.5:*** In professional relationships the practical meaning of communication is the response you get.
>
> ***Principle 3.6:*** When there is consistent and accurate feedback during the professional relationship, clients will become increasingly responsible for themselves.

Science and Art Combined. Building effective professional relationships is both a science and an art and consequently has characteristics of both. From a scientific perspective, effective professionals maintain an objective posture, building toward goals through the development of effective interpersonal relationships. Effective relationships are orderly and sequential, with stages of the process building upon one another. In addition to scientific elements, effective professional relationships incorporate a high degree of art. Art refers to the unique and creative ways individual professionals apply scientific elements to each client relationship.

This merging of scientific and artistic elements is analogous to the painting of a picture. Although there are scientific principles for mixing a color palette and applying paint to the canvas, art in painting comes from the unique way artists apply paints to create images. The same is true in professional relationships—professionals artistically use scientific principles.

Principle 3.1: *The purpose of professional relationships is to influence and motivate.* All professional relationships in the financial arena have the general purpose of influencing and motivating clients. The form and amount of influence attempted will change with the unique purpose of the professional relationship, but influence and motivation are at the core of all professional relationships.

Communication is reciprocal—what one person says has an effect on the type of response that will be made. Because of the reciprocal nature of communication, one cannot *not* influence. Whether we intend to or not, the way we communicate or the manner in which we choose to respond has an effect on the way people respond to us.

In professional financial relationships the influence we exert results from this reciprocity as well as from our desire to influence the client toward some goal. Influence varies along a continuum from a sales presentation to remedial financial counseling. In the sales presentation, the goal of our influence is to convince a client to buy a product or service. In remedial financial counseling, the counselor usually deals with clients who are financially overextended. These are clients who have made irresponsible decisions about their money. In remedial financial counseling, the purpose of influence is to move clients to make responsible financial decisions for themselves. While our specific goals may vary, our underlying purpose remains constant—to influence.

There are many ways to influence. One's ability to influence rests on four major elements. The first is an understanding of how people process information. This was discussed in Chapter 1. The second issue is the financial professional's sources of personal power, which will be discussed in Chapter 4. A third element is the effective use of the communication environment. The final issue deals with how to control the communicative relationship. Effective financial professionals utilize specific communicative skills to control their professional relationships.

There are two aspects to control. We can control process and we can control content of information. In reality, content and process overlap; they are separated here only for discussion. Financial professionals are primarily responsible for process, and clients are primarily responsible for content. While content affects process and *vice versa*, the focus of the financial professional's influence should be on process, influencing how information is dealt with. Clients, on the other hand, focus on content: the information necessary for understanding, problem solving, goal setting, and decision making.

It is entirely possible for a financial professional to control a process and help clients move toward problem solving or decision making without knowing any of the information the client is using. For example, a financial professional might conduct a planning seminar for a group of clients. During the seminar the financial professional could guide clients through a planning process: through completing a net worth statement, through writing several financial goals for the next six months, through listing possible ways of achieving the goals, through making a choice among the various alternatives, and through developing a personal plan to implement chosen alternatives to achieve goals. Each client would supply necessary information and develop an action plan, while the financial professional would have no knowledge of individual content used. In this type of seminar the financial professional controls the process, and clients control the content.

> ⋙**FOCUS ON PROCESS** → This example is used to illustrate that the financial professional's primary responsibility is to control the process of interaction as a means for exerting influence. The remaining principles in this chapter deal with this concept.

Principle 3.2: *Six dimensions exist in an ideal professional relationship: openness, realistic expectations, structure, power, confirmation of differences, and mutual involvement*. Effective professional relationships usually incorporate most, if not all, of these six dimensions at one time or another. Although each of the dimensions is discussed separately here, keep in mind that they are interactive.

Openness. Openness refers to individuals' willingness to share information about the topic under discussion and about personal aspects that relate to the purpose of the relationship. One way of understanding the concept of openness is through the metaphor of the Johari window (see Figure 3.A). The Johari window is named after Joe Luft and Harry Ingram, who originally conceived of using a four-pane window as a way of expressing the areas and degrees of openness appropriate in communicative relationships.

Figure 3.A

	Known to self	**Not known to self**
Known to others	**Public**	**Blind**
Not known to others	**Private**	**Hidden**

Here's how the Johari window works:

▶ In normal communication the nature of the information dealt with is in the *public* area: information that is known to both persons. This is the type of information that we share readily with others and that they share with us.

▶ The *private* area contains two differing types of information. The first type of information relates to things about oneself, such as values, beliefs, fears, and feelings that are shared only with certain people or under certain circumstances. The second type of information contained in the *private* area relates to reactions to others during the communicative interaction. We have feelings, judgments, and ideas about others which we are aware of but may not share with others.

▶ In a similar manner, the information in a person's *blind* area relates to others' reactions, feelings, judgments, and ideas about him or her which they do not readily share.

▶ The information contained in the *hidden* area relates to deeper subconscious processes that are not readily available to the individual or to others as they communicate. We can become aware of information in the *hidden* area through dreams, either night dreams or daydreams; in moments of emergency; through free association; through therapy; and so on.

Openness in professional relationships refers to your willingness to share with the client information from your *private* area and his or her willingness to share with you information from his or her *private* area. Information from the *private* area that is most appropriate to share in professional financial relationships relates to your judgments, ideas, and reactions to the client. There are times when it also may be important to share your beliefs, values, and judgments about financial issues relevant to the purpose of the professional relationship. You also may wish to create an atmosphere in which clients are willing to self-disclose information. Open communicative relationships can be depicted as follows (see Figure 3.B):

Figure 3.B

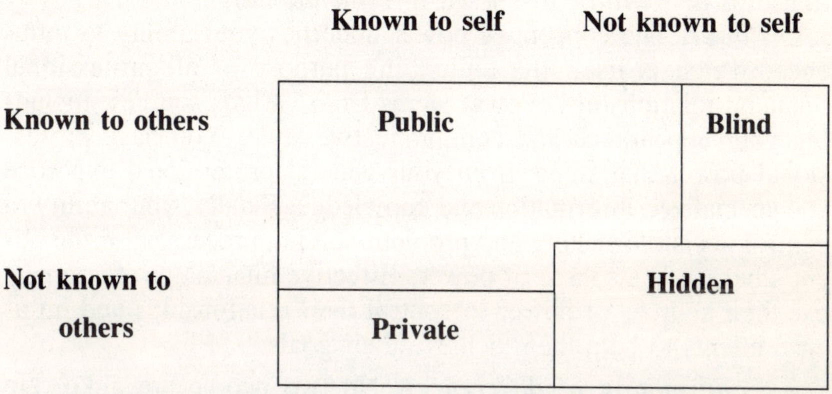

Notice that as one person shares information from the *private* area, this area gets smaller, and so does the *blind* area. This occurs because as people share their feelings, reactions, and judgments about other people, each becomes more aware of things that were previously known only to the other. Notice also that as the self-disclosure continues, the *public* area becomes larger. This is the nature of open relationships.

Realistic Expectations. There are two aspects of realistic expectations to keep in mind.

▸ *Client goals.* The judgment as to whether goal expectations are realistic or not depends upon a number of factors in the relationship. In any given situation, you will need to exercise knowledge and experience to determine if specific goals are realistic.

▸ *Client expectations for you and your role.* Some clients may expect you to take complete control of their financial situation and to make all the necessary decisions. This may be applicable if you are setting up a trust to be managed by you or your institution. On the other hand, it may be unrealistic for clients to expect that you will make their decisions for them. In either case, effective financial professionals spend time at the beginning of their working relationships to clarify role expectations so that there are no misunderstandings later.

Structure. Effective professional relationships follow a structure appropriate to the setting and the goals of the relationship. We referred to such a structure at the beginning of the chapter when we discussed the scientific and artistic nature of effective relationships. There is an underlying structure to effective professional relationships that will be discussed in Principle 3.3.

Power. The concept of power underlies your ability to influence, which is itself the underlying purpose of all professional financial relationships. Power stems from various sources, including your appearance and communicative style. You have professional power that stems from your general professional expertise and specialized information and knowledge. Finally, your ability to control decision-making and problem-solving processes for the client's benefit is a source of power. Effective financial professionals use their sources of power to control their relationships and influence clients to help them achieve their goals.

Confirmation of differences. No two people are alike. No doubt you and your clients will differ about financial values, beliefs, and attitudes; willingness to take financial risks; financial goals; and so on. Effective financial professionals recognize these differences, help their clients to understand what they are, and help clients to use their understanding to make personally relevant choices. This approach is in direct contrast to attempting to make clients behave or choose as you might. When you try to influence clients to do things your way, it may be perceived as a "hard sell," and clients will look elsewhere for the help they need.

There is a delicate balance that must be maintained. Although you need to share with clients your best judgments, you must recognize that achieving their goals will be most directly related to their qualities, values, and beliefs. There is potential conflict when a major difference exists between you and your clients. Conflict may arise especially when client goals are unrealistic, given their values and beliefs. For example, clients may wish to become financially independent in a short period of time but want only "safe" or "guaranteed" investments. In such a situation it is appropriate for you to point out the discrepancy by giving appropriate feedback. However, you should avoid trying to persuade the client to be a greater risk taker. Confirming differences and operating within them builds the trust necessary for effective professional financial relationships.

Mutual involvement. This concepts relates to realistic expectations. The most effective relationships occur when both parties actively attempt to make the relationship satisfying while planning for and achieving goals. Underlying this concept is the issue of dependence. When clients become too dependent upon you, allowing or wanting you to make all of their decisions for them, you become totally responsible for their goals. If something you suggest does not produce the results either you or the client desire, then you are "at fault" for failure. The key to effective relationships is to get clients involved as much as possible so that there is mutual responsibility for setting goals and developing plans to achieve them.

Again, the six dimensions of an ideal professional relationship are interrelated. As openness develops in the relationship, the likelihood increases that expectations will become more realistic and differences will be acknowledged and accepted. Finally, the degree of mutual involvement is related to the degree of openness. As you and the client become more self-disclosing and your public areas become progressively larger, the greater will be your mutual involvement.

Principle 3.3: *Professional relationships progress through four stages: initiating, exploring, understanding, and acting.* Because effective professional financial relationships do not happen magically, understanding the four developmental stages will provide a basis for increasing your ability to control the process.

Initiating. The initial moments of any professional relationship include the client's perception of friendliness, threat, and responsiveness. The initial criteria of friendliness usually are not hard to meet. A smile, a firm handshake, direct eye contact, and a warm greeting all communicate an interested attitude. Small talk, even about the weather or recent newsworthy events, helps reduce the tension associated with beginning or renewing a professional relationship. The purpose of the small talk is to help both you and the client relax and to create a readiness to begin.

You may not see yourself as a threat to a client. After all, you want to help clients make the best use of their finances or help people overcome financial problems in their lives. But keep in mind that, to some degree, you are an intruder in the client's life. You will be an unknown until the professional relationship is firmly established. Finances are a personal matter, and talking about them may pose a number of possible threats to clients. Consciously or subconsciously, clients want to know certain things about the financial professional. Will this person think I have made foolish decisions with my money? Will the person understand what I want? Will this person try to "sell" me something? How do I know this person can be trusted? These and other questions pose varying degrees of threat for clients as they initiate a professional relationship with you. It's up to you to be as nonthreatening as possible.

Finally, you should be a good listener and responsive, especially at the beginning of a relationship. You can demonstrate that you are a good listener by actively attending to what clients have to say through the use of a variety of communication skills. Active listening can demonstrate to clients that you are interested in them, that you appreciate the feelings, even fear, they reveal, and that you want to assist them in whatever way is appropriate for the professional relationship.

People have various motivations for initiating relationships, with the motivations often being different from goals. While goals refer to potential outcomes, motivations refer to the nature of relationships people desire. Professional financial relationships can vary on a continuum from "strictly business" to close, personal friendships. People do not always start professional relationships with a particular motivation. Professional relationships develop over time and, based on the experience between the people involved, move along the continuum. The degree of initial openness and friendliness both you and the client express sets a tone for your continued relationship. During this stage, each person constructs a picture, consciously or subconsciously, of the other person. Even though this picture is continuously subject to change, the picture is used as a basis for continued communication. As people communicate, they may discover that they have certain interests in common and as a result become more interested in each other. The more similar you and the client are in interests, values, and beliefs, the more likely the relationship will move along the continuum toward a personal friendship.

⋙**BEWARE THE TOO FRIENDLY**→ It is neither possible nor desirable for you to become personal friends with each of your clients. You should be aware of two potential problems as your relationships develop. First, the client may wish the relationship to develop beyond "strictly business" to friendship, while you are trying to keep the relationship focused on the initial goal or purpose. Second, if a professional relationship does develop into a friendship, it may be difficult to remain objective when dealing with business issues.

Exploring. Once the professional relationship has been initiated either as a new relationship or as part of a continuing relationship, the next stage is to explore important issues relating to the client's needs, purposes, or goals. There are times when the initiation of the professional relationship is by the client. At other times, you may have initiated the relationship or interview. You should be aware that sometimes clients may use the small talk appropriate in initiating an interview or relationship as a way of avoiding exploring important issues. There are two aspects to exploring which are not necessarily mutually exclusive: planning and problem solving.

When the general purpose of your professional relationship is *planning*, the focus of exploring is on needs and goals. Client goals can vary from very complex issues that involve a great deal of exploring to immediate decisions about financial issues that involve very little exploring. Exploring in the planning situation may involve your acquiring additional information from or for the client. For example, in estate planning you need to know everything relevant to the client's financial situation, needs, and ultimate goals—information that comes from the client. On the other hand, the client may want more information about an investment opportunity, information which you need to research and then share with the client. This is information you would have to gather for the client. In essence, you have to be able to gather information within and outside the relationship, and to use both types in behalf of the client.

In a situation where the general purpose is *problem solving*, the financial professional relationship takes on characteristics of a helping relationship. The following questions are helpful in problem-solving situations.

▸*Is the presented problem the real problem?* Many times clients may not reveal the real problem until they are comfortable that you are someone who can be trusted. In addition they may withhold the real problem, not because of lack of trust, but because they themselves are not sure of what the real problem is.

▸ *Is the presented problem a solution to some other problem?* An effective way of looking at problems is as solutions to other problems. In the financial arena, it seems likely that there are few financial problems that aren't solutions to other things. It is difficult to imagine someone not knowing that spending more money than they have will create financial problems for them. If this is such an obvious connection, then why would someone do something which seems so self-defeating? It is usually because they are using money to solve some other problem or to meet some other need, like "trying to keep up with the Joneses." In this type of situation clients may have high status needs and purchase things to fulfill those needs. Eventually they will become financially over-extended. The real problem is not the money but their use of money to gain social approval.

▸ *What type of problem is it?* Some possibilities might be a conflict of personal values, unrealistic goals, or lack of information.

▸ *Who owns the problem?* Make sure it is the client's problem. If it isn't, then it changes your role to that of a consultant in helping the client to help others.

▸ *What solutions has the client tried thus far?* Knowing this gives you information about the client's problem-solving and decision-making processes and tells you what not to suggest to avoid a response that begins with "Yes, but. . . ." If you suggest a solution the client has tried before to no avail, clients may become defensive and resist other good solutions.

▸ *What financial and personal resources does the client have?* Financial resources relate to the client's financial worth, while personal resources relate to the client's use of personal abilities to achieve stated goals. Clients may have personal resources that they have not used to solve the presented problem. For example, a woman may not think she has financial management skills. This same woman may have been managing all of her family's finances or managing the finances for a church group. This client may have been using many of the skills in her personal life that would help her achieve the goals she would like to achieve working with you.

Answers to these and other questions are important in the exploring stage of professional relationships dealing with financial problems. The purpose of the exploring stage is to gather the information necessary to move to the developmental stage in professional relationships.

Understanding. This stage of the professional financial relationship is when you and the client generate plans for either goal achievement or problem solving. The type of plans will vary with the type of financial relationship. Emphasis during this stage should be upon generating at least three possible alternatives. There are a number of ways that alternatives can be generated.

- ▶You, the financial professional, may suggest alternatives.
- ▶You can encourage the client to generate the alternatives.
- ▶Both you and the client can generate the alternatives.

Generating a number of possible alternatives allows the client to make a choice, which in turn makes the client responsible for any of the outcomes of the choice. Allowing the client to make the choice prevents the possibility that the client may blame you if the alternative doesn't work the way the client hoped. If the understanding stage proceeds as expected, there is a natural evolution to the final stage.

Acting. During the action stage you or the client begin carrying out the alternatives chosen during the understanding stage. A necessary part of the action stage is the ongoing evaluation of how well the alternatives are working either to achieve the established goals or to solve the problems. If evaluation results indicate that goals are not being achieved, then you and the client can return to earlier stages of exploring or understanding.

A primary reason why alternatives fail to produce desired results is that information gathered during the exploring stage may have been incomplete or not appropriate for the situation. The possibility also exists that you and the client moved to the understanding stage too quickly. It usually is better to err by spending too much time in the exploratory stage than by spending too little. It is extremely important that you and the client are certain that you have discussed all the pertinent information. Delaying alternatives generation until all information has been discussed will be helpful in the long run.

Principle 3.4: ***Specific professional financial relationships have specific developmental stages.*** Professional financial relationships vary according to their purpose. While the four basic developmental stages discussed under Principle 3.3 underlie most professional financial relationships, there are some that have specific developmental stages. Several are outlined below to indicate how the broader developmental stages need to be adapted to specific purposes.

Financial Planning Model. The financial planning model has six stages.

1. *Gathering data.* Accurate, pertinent data is the essence of financial planning. There are two kinds of important data: quantitative and qualitative. Quantitative data is the usual factual information of the client's financial situation: data relating to assets, liabilities, income, expenditures, and so on. Qualitative data is the basis for understanding the client's representational map about issues which affect financial planning: money values, financial goals, financial decision-making style, learning style, general and financial risk taking, social and psychological needs, and family relationships.

2. *Establishing client objectives.* Using both quantitative and qualitative data, the financial planner helps clients establish realistic objectives that are an outgrowth of their experiential maps and based on stated goals.

3. *Processing and analyzing information.* The financial planner must be skilled in processing and analyzing two types of information. The first, of course, is the technical information. Based upon a definitive understanding of economics and the nuances of time and its influence on the value of money, the financial planner must be able to provide clients realistic insights about technical information like financial statements, legal contracts, stocks, bonds, mutual funds, investment contracts, and real estate issues. Appropriate advice, however, is equally dependent on the second required area of knowledge, knowledge about clients. Most would agree that one financial plan will not fit all clients' needs or that one financial plan will not meet an individual client's needs for all time. People are different and people change.

4. *Recommending a total plan.* Before financial planners can recommend a total financial plan, they must take every precaution that all viable alternatives have been explored; that proposed choices are indeed appropriate to the client's constraints and

goals; and that all information concerning the client's needs and goals have been explored. Once the financial planners are satisfied that all significant possibilities have been examined, they can recommend a total financial plan. This stage, the recommendation of a plan, perhaps is the most crucial because at this point the client is given the integrated data the financial planner brings to bear on the client's situation. The goal of this stage is to bring the client's experiential map together with a financial plan—a plan designed specifically to meet the client's needs and developed to achieve the client's objectives.

5. *Implementing the plan.* Once the plan is recommended and accepted by the client, implementation can occur. Implementation usually occurs in one of two ways. In situations where the financial planner has expertise and appropriate credentials, the financial planner can implement the plan directly. In other cases, however, the financial planner must be able to work in a liaison capacity with other financial planning professionals: accountants, insurance agents, brokers, and attorneys.

6. *Monitoring the plan.* The final stage is a continuous process of evaluation and subsequent modification to assure that the financial plan, as devised and implemented, continues to operate in the client's best interests. When significant changes occur in either the marketplace or clients' lives, the six-stage model automatically recycles to the first stage, *Gathering data*.

Financial counseling model. Financial counseling, like financial planning, usually has six stages. The major difference between the two models lies in focus or goals. Financial counseling emphasizes remedial, preventive, and productive issues, whereas financial planning focuses almost exclusively on clients' productive goals. The six stages of financial counseling are as follows.

1. *Building a relationship.* The financial counseling relationship depends upon the counselor's skill in conveying a positive attitude to clients, and an awareness of their financial situations, and in conveying concern in a helpful and beneficial way. The underlying purpose of financial counseling is to help clients help themselves to solve or prevent financial problems. "If I

give you fish, I have fed you for today; if I teach you how to fish, I have fed you for a lifetime.'' This old adage incorporates the underlying purpose of financial counseling. The effective financial counseling relationship is characterized by the four core conditions of congruence, empathy, warmth, and trust.

▸Congruence refers to the financial counselor's consistency, genuineness, and honesty. Congruent communication requires that both verbal and nonverbal behaviors are consistent.

▸Empathy is the financial counselor's ability to put himself or herself into the client's frame of reference and to understand the client's representational map as the client understands it. Empathy also includes the ability to share this understanding with the client in an objective, third-party attitude so that the financial counselor can bring a detached logic to bear on the financial problem.

▸Warmth includes the financial counselor's friendliness, openness, and consideration.

▸Trust is critical in financial counseling. Trust is based on the client's belief that the financial counselor is working in his or her best interest. Trust results from the financial counselor's ability to genuinely demonstrate openness, congruence, empathy, and warmth.

2. *Diagnosing needs and setting goals.* Diagnosis is a systematic attempt to understand clients and their financial situation. A good diagnosis is a description of a client's problem which includes essential details of the problem, its history, and possible causes. The answers to the questions raised in the exploring stage, discussed under Principle 3.3, are the basis of effective diagnosis.

   Goal setting is the logical outcome of diagnosis. Goals in financial counseling revolve around two major areas. The first are process goals which state how the financial counselor intends to help clients. The second are outcome goals, which specify what clients will be doing differently with their finances as a result of the help received in financial counseling.

3. *Generating of alternatives.* In financial counseling it is important that the counselor establish an attitude that clients have the

potential for accomplishing their own goals. One way of doing this is to help clients generate their own alternatives. Financial counselors often suggest some possible solutions. However, clients are more likely to carry out alternatives they have discovered for themselves than those suggested by other people. Helping clients generate their own alternatives serves another broader purpose. If an alternative does not work, clients must take personal responsibility and not blame the financial counselor.

4. *Choosing a plan of action.* Once possible solutions are generated, the financial counselor helps clients to evaluate alternatives in light of diagnosed needs and the established goals. Effective financial counselors can pose pertinent questions. What are the costs and benefits of each alternative? (Costs and benefits refer to more than just finances. Costs and benefits include effort, emotional stress, social factors, time factors, psychological factors, and even physical considerations.) What could possibly go wrong if an alternative is used? What is the potential impact of the alternative not working? Answers to these and similar questions help clients and financial counselors narrow down which alternatives may best meet the diagnosed needs and goals.

5. *Implementing the plan.* At this stage the emphasis is upon action. The client and financial counselor must do something to carry out the alternatives chosen to solve the problem. This is usually accomplished by answering the questions: Who does what, when, and where. Responsibilities are assigned and schedules are established to carry out the plan.

6. *Evaluating the plan.* In financial counseling there are two areas for evaluation: the process and the outcomes. When evaluating the process, financial counselors are concerned with the problem-solving process they and clients used during the previous six stages. Financial counselors are concerned that clients learn a process they can use to help themselves in the future.

⋙**GOAL IS SELF-RELIANCE** → Financial counseling differs in this regard from financial planning. One of the goals of financial counselors is to work themselves out of business with their clients. That is, if they do their work effectively, their clients will no longer need them and will be able to solve their own problems in the future because they have learned a process they can apply by themselves.

Of course, financial counselors also evaluate outcomes. Did the client actually carry out the plan and solve the problem? In both forms of evaluation, there may be the need to recycle through some of the stages until both counselor and client are satisfied that mutual goals have been accomplished.

A sales model of interaction. Sales, like financial planning and financial counseling, is orderly and purposeful. Four stages are readily apparent in this sequential process.

1. *Initiating*. In this stage the professional must initiate or establish a relationship. This process can be begun by either the professional or the client. In both cases it is of utmost importance that the professional establish a relationship that is based on trust and sincerity. Elements discussed earlier under previous models also apply here. For example, the sales professional must demonstrate good listening skills; must be responsive to client wants, needs, and desires; must be empathic, genuine, and honest; and must be consistent in verbal and nonverbal communication. In addition to these relationship variables, the sales professional must communicate to clients the purpose for the interaction and what the client will gain from participation. It is important that the sales professional establish a need for involvement in the client's mind, in order to move to the next stage.

2. *Exploring*. In the exploration stage the salesperson must acknowledge and account for the client's needs and goals. The client's needs may be specifically stated; however, this is the exception rather than the rule. Most clients have a vague idea of what they would like and look to the salesperson for details that will help them to clarify their needs. In order to help clients to understand their needs and to specify their goals, salespersons must be able to help clients explore all aspects of their impending purchase. It is crucial at this point for the salesperson to focus on clients' needs and to hold in abeyance any desires for personal gain or profit. The exploration stage should be used to help clients to achieve clarity and specificity and will end when goals have been established.

3. *Acting*. This stage has two primary aspects: examining possible alternatives and establishing plans for achieving goals. There may be many ways to achieve the client's goals. The salesperson can help the client to generate alternative means for achieving goals and provide assistance in determining the costs and benefits for alternatives. In this stage salespersons are cautioned to examine costs and benefits of alternatives from a broad perspective. That is, salespersons should help clients to think about financial, social, time, emotional, and physical aspects of possible alternatives. Once all of these aspects have been examined, salespersons can help clients to decide which of several options they would like to exercise.

4. *Closing*. Closing has three primary components: satisfying clients, eliciting clients' commitment, and following through on choices made by clients. In all three of these, salespersons must communicate that their purpose is to help clients to meet their original needs and to achieve those goals that were determined to be important. All three of these final components are important for immediate client satisfaction, for ensuring that clients will expend the effort and other resources needed to accomplish their goals, and to set the stage for future client-salesperson interactions.

Principle 3.5: *In professional relationships the practical meaning of communication is the response you get*. As discussed in Chapter 1, communication between you and your clients is a reciprocal relationship. What you say or do with a client will affect what kind of response you will receive from the client and *vice versa*. Usually whatever you did to get a response will produce the same or a similar response if you do it again. Yet, frequently it appears that the communicator's intention or motivation is independent of the response elicited. Most people have had the experience of saying something innocent to someone and getting a response of frustration or anger. The original intention was to engage in conversation, but the second person responded as if the first person had purposely tried to frustrate or anger him or her. In this type of situation, the practical meaning of the communicative interaction is the response of the second person, not the first person's innocent motivation. What needs to be dealt with in a productive way is the response.

An example from everyday life might clarify this principle. A couple's young son is not behaving according to expectations. The child is not spending an appropriate amount of time studying, is not cleaning up his room, and is not helping around the house. In this situation, the parents may use a lecture approach. They may sit down and talk with the child and explain their expectations, explain why it is important, and try to motivate the child with a "pep talk." Much to their chagrin, they find that their child continues to act in the same way. They again talk with the child, but this time they express their anger and frustration. The child continues to act in the same way. The parents try again, with more anger and frustration and even a few four-letter expletives! The child still doesn't change. In this situation the parents continued to try the same tactic (talking) over and over again. Each time they received an identical response. The practical point of this principle is that if you aren't getting the response you want, then try something different. For example, the frustrated parents might try denying the child some privilege to enforce change.

There are two underlying assumptions in this principle. The first is that you do have some idea of the type of response you want from clients. The second is that you must have a variety of communicative skills to produce different responses. You should also have a number of approaches for explaining the same concept or presenting the same information. Most of us have had the experience of having people explain something to us and when we indicate that we don't understand what they are trying to tell us, to have them repeat what they said originally, but in a slower and more precise manner. When they explain it again in the same way, it doesn't help any more than it did the first time! Chapters 5, 6, and 7 have been developed to help you overcome this difficulty; they describe a number of communication skills that can be used to add variety to your approach.

Principle 3.6: *When there is consistent and accurate feedback during the professional relationship, clients will become increasingly responsible for themselves.* Communication is a process of making informational outputs and receiving informational inputs. Feedback is a special class of interactive information processing. Technically, feedback is a specific kind of input people use for correcting their informational outputs. Feedback is simply a process in which some of a person's informational output is returned to the person as part of new informational input. Feedback is an essential form of information processing because it allows people to become more self-directing, or responsible for themselves. When people have feedback about their outputs relative to their goals, they can make appropriate corrections to achieve their goals.

The simplest mechanical example of a self-directing feedback system is the automatic thermostat. When a thermostat is set at a specific temperature, a goal is established. When the temperature in a house falls below the prescribed temperature, the thermostat provides feedback to the furnace through an electrical signal. The furnace responds, turns on, and supplies heat to the house. When the temperature reaches the desired level, the thermostat gives feedback to the furnace that the goal has been achieved, and the furnace turns off. This simple mechanical system will continue to achieve its goal until a mechanical or electrical failure destroys the feedback process. The thermostat can be said to be a self-directing system. We can say that the thermostat is *responsible for itself* in the sense that it continues to achieve its goal to control the temperature in the house without any input from the outside.

People operate in a similar manner. When they receive feedback they become more self-directing and responsible for themselves relative to their goals. Feedback can be positive, negative, constructive, or destructive.

▸ *Positive* feedback provides information to people that their behavior is consistent with their goals, thus encouraging them to continue behaving in ways that will help them to achieve their goals. Positive feedback may also tell people that they have achieved a goal and allows them to establish new goals.

▸ *Negative* feedback operates in a restricting manner, tending to keep people within the limits prescribed by their goals. Negative feedback provides people with information that their behavior is not consistent with goals. In effect, it provides people with information about how far they are from achieving their goals.

▸ Feedback is *constructive* if it is used to help people measure whether their behavior is helping them to achieve their goals.

▸ If feedback is used to discourage or belittle people, it is *destructive*.

Obviously, financial professionals should make a concerted effort to use constructive feedback and encourage their clients to do the same. Much of effective communication between you and your clients relies on the transmission of feedback. Keeping the following few points in mind will help you in providing appropriate feedback.

▶ Focus feedback on behavior rather than on the person. Making a statement like, "You aren't very responsible with your money," focuses on the person and makes a judgment about him or her. On the other hand, making a statement like, "Using your credit cards instead of cash is causing some problems," focuses on the person's behavior. The concept to keep in mind is that people can change their behavior more easily than they can alter the qualities we judge them to have. Besides, our judgments may not always be accurate.

▶ Focus feedback on immediate situations. Feedback that is not closely related to behavior is not useful. As discussed above, the purpose of feedback is to help people to achieve their goals. Feedback such as, "You never seem to think ahead," focuses on a judgment made about the person and on some indeterminate time. It might be better to say something like, "You don't seem to be thinking of what will happen if you choose that alternative." Even with feedback, behavior which happened last week or last month cannot be corrected. You cannot change the past. But you can have an effect on the present with your feedback.

▶ Consider the amount of feedback the receiver can use at one time rather than the amount of information you have or want to share. There are times when you have accumulated a great deal of information about a client, information which may be helpful if the client knew about it. However, keep in mind that clients can deal with only a certain amount of information at one time. This is especially true if the feedback you wish to share with clients is negative. Don't overwhelm clients with large quantities of feedback at one time.

▶ Focus on the feedback's potential value for the receiver, not on the value or release it provides you. Feedback, especially negative feedback, can be misused when it is merely a way of venting emotions. Remember, feedback should be offered as a help to the client.

Feedback is an essential process in communication. It is the process that helps people to become more self-directing and responsible for themselves. Effective feedback can help clients to achieve their goals without causing them to feel bad about themselves, their choices, or their behaviors.

CHAPTER 4

The Listening Process

This chapter is about listening and the part that it plays in communication. We will discuss the important dimensions of listening, examine specific rules for the process, and investigate a number of issues that influence how you listen.

Dimensions of listening. Consider the following dialogue between Fred, a realtor who has a vested interest in the sale of a tract of land, and Mary, a potential client.

Realtor: Mary, the land that I've been talking about is the best land of its kind this side of the Mississippi. There is no way that this land won't appreciate tenfold in value. Furthermore, the terms for buying this land are so good that a person would be foolish not to jump at the opportunity of purchasing it. Why, if I had the money, I'd buy this piece in a minute.

Client: Well, I don't know if I'm interested in that kind of property.

Keep in mind that the *words* in the interchange are only the surface of the communication that took place. An integral part of the communication are the *thoughts* that provide a basis for the words. With this example as a backdrop, we can discuss a number of the primary dimensions of listening.

▸ *Attending*. Attending refers to the process of paying attention to internal or external stimuli. We live in a world full of stimuli, some of which are important to us, while others are relatively unimportant. We learn to selectively screen what *is* important from that which is *not* important. This process allows us to function in a manner that is consistent with our personal needs, values, and goals. It allows us to use stimuli that will be helpful to us in our quest for personal satisfaction.

From a negative perspective, selective attention can prevent us from experiencing some elements that are important. In the song "The Sounds of Silence," Simon and Garfunkel capture the essence of this when they refer to ". . . people talking without speaking, people hearing without listening . . ." We frequently hear the words but, unfortunately, do not pay attention to the message. In interactions, selective inattention prevents meaningful communication from occurring.

In our example, Fred could be so intent on convincing Mary about the value of purchasing that he would selectively attend to Mary's response *only* if it agreed with what he wanted. He could miss any response that was inconsistent with his point of view. Thus, he might selectively attend only to the words, "I don't know if I'm interested," which might mean that there is still hope, thus providing some encouragement for him to continue. Mary could also attend selectively. She might believe that salespeople who use a hard-sell approach are untrustworthy. Her tentative reply seems to imply that she thinks Fred is using a hard-sell approach. Once she placed Fred in this category, Mary would attend to Fred's style and would not attend to his message. The result probably would be Mary's rejection of Fred and his suggestions.

▸*Assigning meaning*. Once stimuli are attended to, meaning is assigned. Let's assume Mary attended to Fred's style and determined that Fred was untrustworthy. To arrive at this conclusion, Mary probably compared Fred to other people she has known and to how she has viewed these people. This process of comparison to stored experiences, a portion of her representational map, is the primary method for assigning meaning. To exemplify this, count the triangles in the following drawing (Figure 4.A).

Figure 4.A

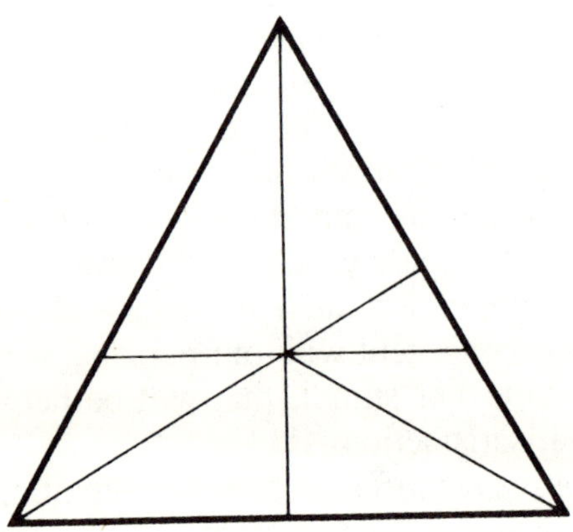

How many triangles did you count? In most instances, people will arrive at an answer of between eight and twelve. However, when all are counted, you will find that there are eighteen. Look at Figure 4.B to see how to find all of them.

Figure 4.B

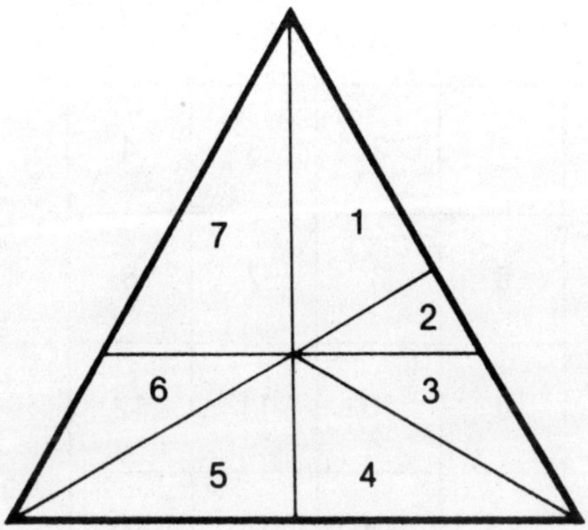

Combinations

1) 1	**7)** 7	**13)** 1+2+7
2) 2	**8)** 1+2	**14)** 5+6+7
3) 3	**9)** 2+3	**15)** 2+3+4+5
4) 4	**10)** 1+2+3	**16)** 6+7
5) 5	**11)** 4+5	**17)** 1+2+3+4
6) 6	**12)** 1+6+7	**18)** 1+2+3+4+5+6+7

It is our assumption that you now have a *new* way of viewing problems like the one presented above and that you can use this new learning as a reference point for a second problem. In the following drawing (Figure 4.C), how many squares can you count?

Figure 4.C

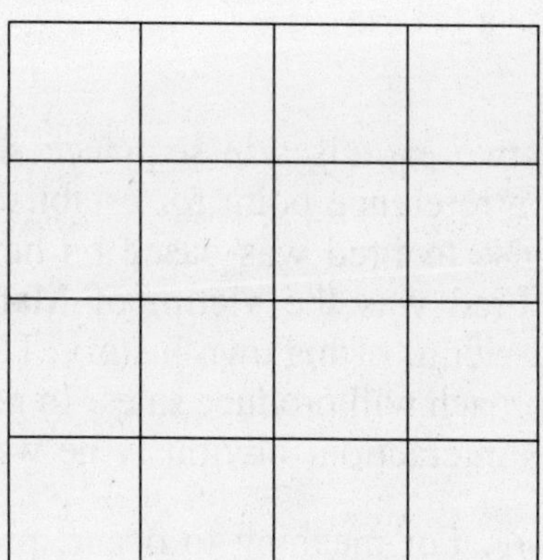

In most cases, people will count more than they would have counted had they not been exposed to the triangle counting problem. There are thirty squares in the second problem. The following drawing (Figure 4.D) can be used to locate them.

Figure 4.D

1	2	3	4
5	6	7	8
9	10	11	12
13	14	15	16

To find the thirty squares you need to form the combinations show below in Figure 4.E.

Figure 4.E. **Combinations**

1) 1	**9)** 9	**17)** 1+2+5+6	**25)** 11+12+15+16
2) 2	**10)** 10	**18)** 5+6+9+10	**26)** 1+2+3+5+6+7+9+10+11
3) 3	**11)** 11	**19)** 9+10+13+14	**27)** 2+3+4+6+7+8+10+11+12
4) 4	**12)** 12	**20)** 2+3+6+7	**28)** 5+6+7+9+10+11+13+14+15
5) 5	**13)** 13	**21)** 6+7+10+11	**29)** 6+7+8+10+11+12+14+15+16
6) 6	**14)** 14	**22)** 10+11+14+15	**30)** 1+2+3+4+5+6+7+8+9+10+11 +12+13+14+15+16
7) 7	**15)** 15	**23)** 3+4+7+8	
8) 8	**16)** 16	**24)** 7+8+11+12	

Solving these two exercises in sequence shows you that experience provides a reference point for establishing meaning.

Mary's response to Fred was based on her previous interactions. In a way, Fred was the victim of Mary's history. Fred, however, is also a victim of his own history. He probably learned that a hard-sell approach will produce sales. In general, he might be correct, but in this interaction, obviously he was wrong.

▸ *Categorizing*. For meaning to occur, previous experiences have to be accessible to the individual. Although it is not clear how data are stored by the human system, it is clear that certain events will evoke categorical responses. Mary's behavior exemplifies this. She responded to Fred in a manner that is similar to how she would or did respond to other salespeople who behaved like Fred. Her thoughts and feelings in her encounter with Fred were immediate and spontaneous. Mary did not have to create a response; rather, her response was automatic and specific to the situation. Stimuli that are attended to are assigned meaning and are categorized according to those specifics of the situation that are similar to stored experiences.

▸ *Remembering*. Remembering, whether conscious or subconscious, is the process of recalling thoughts or feelings about previous occurrences. Without this final dimension, categorization could not occur and meaning would have no reference point.

At times the remembering process is conscious, while at other times it is subconscious. For example, you may consciously try to recall the name of a high school teacher, the title of a favorite movie, or the call letters of a stock on the stock exchange. In most cases, that which you are able to recall will depend on how well you attended to specifics of the original data and on the degree to which you assigned meaning to that data.

The subconscious process of remembering is less predictable but of equal importance. Two key ingredients of subconscious remembering are important.

▸ First, the subconscious process can be set in motion consciously. By using our inherent tendency to finish what is set in motion, we can *program* ourselves or others to use subconscious remembering productively. For example, a lawyer trying to help a client might make the following suggestion, "We've talked about a number of things that you could do to resolve your dilemma. Yet, none of the ideas seems quite right. Instead of continuing to spin our wheels on this, between now and next Thursday when we get together, why don't you think of some other possibilities that don't have the limitations we've discussed." In this example, the lawyer has given the client a conscious message to continue the search for an appropriate solution *and* has provided the client's subconscious a demand—find an appropriate solution to your problem. The lawyer also has set a time limit for the subconscious activity! (More on this issue can be found in Chapter 7.)

▸ A second feature of subconscious processing relates to the use of information stored in our representational maps as a basis for most behavior. As discussed in Chapter 1, our representational maps are a distillation of our previous experiences. These representational maps become the basis for our responses in new situations. This process is most often subconscious and can be best exemplified by our emotional responses. Emotions exist in both conscious and subconscious awareness, but the impact from subconscious remembering frequently is more dramatic. There are many examples in our daily lives. Consider the mother who, upon seeing a college student hug his mother, starts to cry because she misses her son; consider the serviceman who gets tears in his eyes when he hears the Marine Hymn; or consider the moviegoer who alternates between tears and laughter while watching a particularly good movie. Events trigger our memories both consciously and subconsciously.

We have discussed the four dimensions of listening: attending, assigning, meaning, categorizing, and remembering. You either attend or do not attend. In circumstances where you attend, you assign meaning to what is perceived; you classify specifics of the situation; and you remember, consciously and subconsciously, previous experiences that relate to what you attended to. By contrast, what you do not attend to will be lost and not recoverable. Listening, composed of its four dimensions, is the basis for effective communication.

Rules of Listening. *There are a number of rules which, when followed, increase the effectiveness of listening and facilitate communication.*

▸ *Rule one: Respond to the main idea.* In listening to someone, always attempt to determine the person's main message. It is not uncommon for someone to express, through words and actions, a number of messages at one time. As listener, you may have to practice attentiveness and patience to get at the primary message. Consider the following interchange between a marketing expert and a new client.

Client: I've got this new game I'd like you to sell for me. The only thing is, I want to maintain control of who is doing the selling and how much they sell it for. I've tried selling it myself, but I just don't have time.

Agent: Do you want me to sell your game directly, or are you asking me to wholesale it for you?

Client: I want to make sure that I maintain control of what happens to the game and how much it costs.

Agent: So it's not so important to you who sells it, but that whoever does, you want to maintain ultimate control of the game and its price.

Client: That's it.

In this interchange, initially the agent was presented with four ideas: I have a new game; I want control of the game and its price; I've tried to sell the game myself; and I was unsuccessful. The agent's first response to the client seemed to miss the mark. The agent then adjusted his response. The client's "That's it" confirmed that the agent made an appropriate adjustment. This example demonstrates the importance of attending as a dimension of listening. The agent attended to the client. Consequently, she was able to determine the client's main message: "I want to maintain control of the game and its price." The goal for listening should be to understand the sender's message as soon as one can, but, more importantly, to make sure that the main message *is* understood. In the example, this was accomplished.

▸ *Rule two: Respond to emotional messages*. People simultaneously communicate at rational and emotional levels. In business-related communication, usually it is most appropriate for professionals to respond to clients' thoughts. However, since emotions can block rational decisionmaking, financial professionals should listen for indicators of emotions. Consequently, financial professionals must be willing and able to communicate with their clients in a manner that recognizes how emotions affect clients' goals. An example of this point is when an accountant's client states, "I'm afraid of being audited this year." If the client exhibits nervous characteristics that would lead the accountant to believe that the client *is* worried, then it would be appropriate for the accountant to specifically address the client's fears. Failure to address these fears probably would result in ineffective communication and could result in client dissatisfaction and in frustration for the accountant.

▸ *Rule three: Remember significant details.* A good memory is a significant asset in listening and in communication. Clients invariably share a wealth of information relevant to their needs, goals, and circumstances. Effective professionals pay attention to almost everything that is shared, refer to appropriate details in their interactions with clients, and seek clarification of elements that are not clear. The major benefits of this attention to detail are threefold.

▸ Clients will learn to value themselves in professional relationships. Clients will develop the attitude that "my lawyer is paying so much attention to me that she can tell me what I've said, so she must value me." This may seem far-fetched; yet, we probably would agree that if we aren't interested in another person we don't pay close attention. Clients operate from the same frame of reference. They say to themselves, "If you pay attention to what I say, I must be important."

▸ The second significant value in paying attention to detail is that you then have additional information to use in helping clients to achieve their goals. Detail adds flexibility, as we discussed in Chapter 1.

▸ By paying attention to and remembering details, you actively encourage clients to share what is important and relevant to them. In this regard, active listening encourages active client participation.

▸ *Rule four: Make justifiable inferences.* Effective professionals attempt to *make sense* of the data presented to them by clients and share their interpretations with their clients. To do this, you have to be willing to venture educated guesses from the data you have. For instance, a customer, in talking with a car salesperson, states, "I'd like a new car, one that will have a lot of room for the family; one that will get excellent gas mileage." The salesperson might infer that the customer needs a vehicle with significant carrying capacity, but can't afford a large luxury wagon or van. If this is the salesperson's inference, he might say, "Can I assume that you need room in the car you buy, but that you are planning on spending just a moderate amount?" This statement provides the customer with the salesperson's understanding of the situation and allows the customer an opportunity to make adjustments in what has been communicated.

At this point, the customer could respond in a number of ways: "Yes, that about captures my situation" or "Oh no, I really would like a large automobile" or "I guess I haven't really thought about it." In any case, the salesperson will have stimulated the customer, in a nonthreatening manner, to consider what has been communicated. Sharing inferences provides you a means for helping clients understand what has been communicated.

> ⋙**FOLLOW THE RULES→** The rules are straightforward. Effective listening depends on responding to the speaker's main ideas; responding to the speaker's emotional message; remembering significant details of the interaction; and making inferences that are justified by your understanding of your client's situation.

Listening Issues. *Listening is a process that inherently makes you, as a professional, responsible. When someone shares ideas or feelings with you, you are responsible. For professionals, responsibility comes with the territory.* Professionals cannot escape responsible action. The issues highlighted in this section acknowledge the professional responsibility and are included to help you understand subtle areas of responsibility in communications and to alert you to obvious areas where responsibility in listening can be anticipated.

▸*Candor.* How honest should one be in a professional interaction? The answer that immediately comes to mind is, "I should be totally honest!" Yet, when we examine this, it becomes apparent that we can't be totally open or honest in all situations. The closer we look at this issue, the more apparent it becomes that in thinking about honesty, we also must consider balance.

Balance refers to the professional need for maintaining harmony between what you hear, what you feel or believe, and what you say. For instance, a client may say to his financial planner, "All stockbrokers are crooks!" If the financial planner says to the client, "Yeah, I think you are right," he or she may be stating something that, in fact, he or she doesn't believe to be true. If, on the other hand, the financial planner says, "No, I think you are wrong when you say that," the financial planner runs the risk of alienating the client and of destroying harmony or balance in the relationship. In most situations of this type, your best tack is to try to understand the client's emotional message and to *say nothing* or deal with the emotion directly. The financial planner could respond, "You sound angry at stockbrokers. Did you have a bad experience with one?'' The financial planner can then explore the client's experience for information which may be relevant to his or her relationship with the client.

A candid response to a client's question is appropriate when a client specifically asks for your opinion, when your response can shed new light on the topic being discussed, or when there is a legal, ethical, or professional rationale for your input. A candid response may be inappropriate, however, in those situations in which the client is expressing a personal opinion, value, need, or goal. The client who stated, ''All stockbrokers are crooks!'' was *not* asking a question. Rather, he seemed to be stating a value, and this does not require verification from the financial planner.

Both candor and harmony are important. Yet, maintaining a balance between the two may be difficult. When in doubt, you should consider the appropriateness of any response. Consider as a first option not responding at all. As a second option, you may want to deal with the emotional content in your response.

▸ *Deception*. The word ''deception'' automatically has negative connotations. Because of this, you might say to yourself, ''I would never use deception in my professional interactions.'' This may be true for you, but most people say or do things that could be classified as deceptive. Have you ever felt or believed one thing, but said another? Have you ever tried to hide how you felt about a particular issue? Have you ever told a ''little white lie''? Have you ever communicated by omission? If your answer to any of these questions is yes, you have been guilty of deception.

How does deception relate to listening and professional relationships? In communication, there are many occasions for you, as a professional, to listen to your clients. Certainly there are times in these interchanges in which you find your client's comments to be interesting or stimulating. There may be other times, however, in which you find it difficult to pay attention to what your client is saying. What do you do when you find it hard to pay attention? On some occasions, you fight your natural tendency to let your mind wander and force yourself to focus on your client. There probably are those occasions, however, when you succumb to your desire and, for a while, you lose contact with your client. You may pretend to be in contact, but in reality you are not paying attention. This *pretended attention* is a subtle form of deception. It is normal, and if not extreme, of little influence in the relationship. You should be cautioned, however, that if this form of deception becomes too prevalent, your professional relationship will deteriorate and may cease to exist.

A second, more serious issue is related to listening and deception. If, as a professional, you pay attention to your clients selectively, you will be practicing deception. Said another way, if you listen for what you want to hear, and selectively fail to hear what you don't want to hear, you will be acting deceptively. An example may clarify this point. Bill, an encyclopedia salesperson, had a conversation with Lennie, a prospective buyer, about the value of his encyclopedia. The conversation went like this:

Bill: These books will provide you and your family all you'll need to know about many topics for years to come.

Lennie: I appreciate what you have to offer, but I'm a little concerned about making sure the information I have is current.

Bill: I'm glad to see that you value encyclopedias and all the information that they carry.

Lennie: Oh, I do value them, and I think that it is important that my kids have access to current, valid information.

Bill: Good! My company has done an excellent job of getting information from all of the best possible sources. Our encyclopedias are the best, most informative in the business.

And so on.

This second form of deception uses listening as a process for finding out client needs, wants, and so on, and then uses deception—possibly by omission, as done above—to avoid issues that may be important. Deception of this type is unethical and can destroy a professional relationship.

One final aspect of deception should be noted. Clients may interpret your behavior as being deceptive if they observe significant discrepancies between your words and your actions. When someone says one thing but behaves in a contradictory manner, observers frequently conclude that they are being deceived. To avoid the possibility of such an interpretation you should try to be consistent in your verbal and nonverbal communication.

▸*Shared information*. Professionals, through the process of listening, are exposed to a wealth of information about their clients. Some of what professionals learn is through direct client interactions. Some of their knowledge is a result of working with others in the clients' behalf. Still other information, usually of a more subtle nature, is gained from professionals' observations of their clients as they work with them. All information, no matter how it is gained, is private information. Because of the nature of professional relationships, professionals are obligated to maintain client confidentiality and to shield information shared within the professional relationship. Two specific issues related to shared information are important. First, professionals must maintain confidences. Second, professionals must learn ways of handling client secrets. Let's consider each.

1. *Keeping confidences.* Clients frequently share their opinions with professionals. It is important that they have an opportunity to do so. It is equally important that professionals treat all information in a confidential, protective manner. This is important for at least two reasons. First, information is shared under the assumption (by the client) that it will be confidential. A release or sharing of information, without the client's consent, will break the client's implicit trust in the relationship. Second, in most professional relationships, it is illegal or, at the very least, unethical to share client information without the client's release. When professionals choose to release information without client consent, they are risking severance of the relationship and, in some cases, may be breaking the law.

2. *Access to secrets.* As trust develops within professional relationships, clients increasingly share significant aspects of their lives. At times, they share information that is personal, private, or confidential. In most cases, the information is pertinent to the purpose of the professional interaction. At other times, however, information provided may go beyond the professional's needs.

   Access to client secrets is a natural occurrence, one that should be anticipated by professionals. Prepare yourself by devising guidelines for dealing with a number of common situations and how they should be handled. These guidelines should incorporate the fact that all materials shared within your professional relationships should be held in confidence, unless the material clearly indicates potential harm to the client or to society.

Most information that is shared will not indicate potential danger to the client or to others. Rather, the information probably will provide you an indication of the client's values. For instance, consider a banker whose customer brags about underpaying his income taxes. The banker may not have any evidence, other than her customer's statement, that any impropriety has been committed. Yet, the banker will have an insight into her customer's value system, one that may cause the banker some concern.

When we listen to others we find out about them. As professionals, we must be prepared to handle information we obtain, know how to respond in a manner that will be helpful to our clients, and maintain our professional integrity.

▸ *Privacy*. Privacy becomes important in professional relationships in two primary ways. First, clients have a right to privacy. Second, professionals also have a right to privacy. We already have discussed aspects of client confidentially, client sharing, and access to client secrets. These, although related to privacy, do not comprise privacy.

Privacy is the inherent right all clients have to reveal about themselves information that they "choose" to reveal. Clients have the "right" to tell professionals what they choose to tell them. What is shared may be insufficient for meaningful action, but, despite this, clients do have this choice. In most professional situations, clients maintain a "private" stance until they develop trust in the professional and in the professional relationship. By using listening in a caring way, you, as a professional, can help foster a trusting relationship in which pertinent information will be shared from the client's private world.

By the nature of your professional relationships, you can be viewed as a model of action. Your clients observe how you function in the relationship and then use these observations as a point of reference for their own behavior. If you readily share your personal ideas or feelings, they will model your self-disclosure. Your clients will thus learn that this style of interaction is acceptable and, consequently, will soon adopt a similar approach in the relationship.

If, by contrast, you are not comfortable in sharing your ideas and feelings, and hesitate to do so, you will model a nonsharing perspective. Clients will observe this and act accordingly. You should not feel obligated to act or behave in a manner that is uncomfortable for you, but you must be aware of the influence of your actions.

Privacy is important for both parties in professional relationships. Listening, and all the aspects of this process, work against keeping ideas and feelings private. You are entrusted with using your skills to build trusting relationships so that shared materials, and the consequent reduction of privacy, are in the best interests of you and your clients.

CHAPTER 5

Basic Communication Skills

In this chapter the concept of pacing is introduced. Nonverbal pacing is a process through which financial professionals can communicate with clients by mirroring their nonverbal behavior. Closely linked to nonverbal behavior, and perhaps a subcategory of it, is pacing relating to tonality, rate, and volume. Verbal pacing involves a number of communicative elements important in effective financial relationships: client content, emotional theme, specificity of language, and congruence. The verbal skills of restatement, paraphrasing, and summarization are defined, explained, and illustrated. The final topic considers advanced pacing skills dealing with learning styles and language levels.

The Importance of Pacing. Both nonverbal and verbal pacing skills can be used to communicate acceptance, warmth, and understanding, and to build the trust necessary for effective relationships. In a study on the effects of nonverbal and verbal pacing, R.J. Storms made tapes of the same client and counselor under four different counseling situations. In the first situation, the counselor did not pace verbally or nonverbally; in the second situation, the counselor paced nonverbally but not verbally; in the third situation, the counselor paced verbally but not nonverbally; and in the fourth, the counselor paced both verbally and nonverbally. Storms then showed the tapes to experienced counselors, to people with minimal training in counseling, and to people with no training in counseling. None of these people had any training in pacing. All individuals were asked to rate the various situations in terms of the counselor's helpfulness, empathy or understanding, and effectiveness. As one might expect, in the situation in which the counselor paced on both the verbal and nonverbal levels, she was rated as significantly more helpful, effective, and empathetic than the situation in which she did not pace at all.

The interesting finding in this research was that when the counselor paced nonverbally but not verbally, she was rated as being as effective as in the situation where she paced both verbally and nonverbally. Nonverbal pacing used alone was also found to be more effective than verbal pacing alone.

Nonverbal Pacing. When one person deliberately paces (matches) another person's behavior, the second person usually reports feeling listened to, understood, and accepted. Nonverbal pacing requires that you *model* or *copy* the nonverbal behavior of the client. In simple terms, if you fold your arms when your client folds his, you are pacing that behavior—arm folding. Because nonverbal pacing is a powerful and effective communication element, you should use it in developing open, honest interaction.

Nonverbal pacing is a normal, natural part of communication. In studies done in England, films taken of people engaged in conversation were studied frame by frame. In these studies, nonverbal behavior between pairs of individuals matched better than 80% of the time. These studies support our intuitive observations about people and how they naturally pace each other.

For example, we all know couples who have lived together for a few years and seem to talk alike, walk alike, and, in general, exhibit many of the same mannerisms. They pace each other. A similar example can be found in how we choose to talk with young children—we pace them. We get down to their physical level when we talk to them. We bend over or get down on one knee. This is a form of nonverbal pacing. (In addition, we use language consistent with their level of understanding. We use simple language, even "baby talk"—we verbally pace them.)

How should you nonverbally pace a client? You might sit the way he sits or use the same gestures he uses. On a very gross level, this kind of mirroring may be distracting to you and to the client. If you are *caught* doing everything they do, clients may think you are making fun of them. The most effective nonverbal pacing takes place at more subtle levels. You might try to breathe at the same rate as the client. You can blink your eyes at a rate similar to the client's. You might assume the same general posture the client does, either sitting or standing. If the client leans forward, you may lean forward also, and so on.

Since most communication takes place on the nonverbal level, nonverbal pacing communicates very strongly—and usually below clients' level of awareness—that you are interested in everything they have to say; that you accept them; and that you want to develop a facilitative working relationship. This acceptance and closeness form the basis for developing trust and understanding necessary for effective long-term relationships.

A second major benefit of nonverbal pacing is that it is the first step in understanding the client's world. Through your nonverbal mirroring, you can get a sense for what it feels like to be inside the client's world. This perspective can facilitate your understanding of the client and the client's needs and goals.

Following are two experiments designed to help you understand and develop the skill of nonverbal pacing:

▸ Engage a colleague in a discussion and attempt to mirror all of his or her nonverbal behavior. After four or five minutes, ask your colleague for a reaction to you and discuss the preceding communication. Were you perceived as being interested? Did your colleague feel understood? Did he or she feel you were developing a relationship that encouraged discussion? One that fostered trust? One that seemed to be open and honest? When you have discussed these and similar questions, share with your colleague what you were doing. Ask if he or she noticed. In most cases, the paced person will not be aware that you mirrored her behavior and yet will feel understood and accepted.

▸ Practice nonverbal pacing each day. Instead of mirroring exactly what another person does, practice subtle levels of breathing, eye blinks, general body orientation, and voice intonation. To begin, you can practice without even engaging in conversation. For example, practice nonverbal pacing while waiting at an airport, bus depot, or other well-populated place. Simply pick someone near you and practice the subtle art of pacing. This form of practice is most effective when done in situations where you can focus your entire attention on nonverbal behavior without having to engage in conversation. To be skilled at this valuable technique, practice nonverbal pacing at very subtle levels until it becomes second nature to you.

Verbal Pacing. Verbal pacing can be as powerful as nonverbal pacing. Verbal pacing skills should be used throughout all stages of your relationship with clients, but they are especially effective during the initial stage.

Most of us can understand at a rate eight to ten times faster than someone else can talk. We can go to a lecture, speech, or sermon, listen to what is being said, and still think about other things. We can take mental side trips: for example, we might think about what we are going to have for dinner that night, imagine what we are going to do after work, or even think about what we need to get done at home. Despite these mental side trips, we can follow and understand the speaker's main thoughts. This listening speed differential allows us to be aware of our mental thoughts and listen to what someone else is talking about at the same time.

Despite this ability, the process can create problems. It is possible that a mental side trip may become more interesting than what the client is saying. When this happens, you pay greater attention to yourself than to your clients. It stands to reason that if you take mental side trips about a previous client, a person you are meeting for lunch, or a client scheduled later in the day, you will allow yourself to get pulled away from your present client. The message is clear. In professional financial meetings, you must put your listening speed differential to work for you by focusing all of your extra attention on the client. You can begin by pacing nonverbally. The nonverbal pacing process forces you to attend to the client. Try this experiment: talk to someone for a few minutes and establish good eye contact. You will find that while you are maintaining good eye contact you will have difficulty thinking about anything other than what the person is saying.

With clients, put your listening speed differential to good use by attending to four elements of communication. (While all four are defined here, only the first two are important in verbal pacing. The final two are discussed in the next chapter as exploring skills.)

▶ *Content*. The specific words, story line, or stated intent of the client.

▶ *Emotional theme*. The client's feelings about what he or she is saying. Usually this can be observed by attending to the client's voice tone, speech rate, and volume.

▶ *Specificity*. Client words, primarily nouns and verbs, which refer to specific things/actions or which are vague and ambiguous.

▶ *Congruence*. The logical consistency between what a client says and how the client says it. Usually, this refers to the consistency between verbal and nonverbal behavior.

It may seem overwhelming that you have to listen to four elements of communication at the same time. Keep in mind, however, that you can comprehend at a rate eight to ten times faster than someone can speak. If you focus all of your attention on the client, you will find that you can, indeed, listen for all four elements at the same time. Also, keep in mind that you already attend to them at an intuitive level. When people communicate in a monotonal voice, with very low volume, and at a slow rate of speech, you probably would ask them, "What's wrong?" You do this without much thought. At one level of awareness you know that they are sad and upset and act appropriately. Consider the following client statement expressed to a financial professional.

Client (in a slightly frustrated tone of voice): I've come to see you because I need to set money aside for retirement, but I'd rather save up for a vacation. I want both but can't see how to get them. What should I do?

The *content* or story line in this client statement is—I need to set money aside for retirement—I'd rather build up a vacation fund—I want both—I can't see how to get both—Tell me what to do.

The *emotional theme* underlying the client statement is understood when we take into account how the client is presenting the story. We must listen to his tone of voice and watch his nonverbal behavior to determine the theme. In this case the theme might be: "I'm frustrated" or "I'm agitated!"

Verbal Pacing Skills. Several specific skills should be developed to improve your ability to pace your clients verbally:

▸*Restating*. Restating is a process in which you repeat what the client has stated but with emphasis on specifics of content. For example, consider the ways you might restate the client's statement about his vacation and retirement needs:

Client (in a slightly frustrated tone of voice): I've come to see you because I need to set money aside for retirement, but I'd rather save up for a vacation. I want both but can't see how to get them. What should I do?

Here's how you might respond:

Restating of content: You've come to see me because you need to set money aside for retirement . . . and you'd rather save for a vacation . . . but you can't see how to do both . . . and finally, you'd like me to tell you what to do.

Restating of theme: You're feeling frustrated about how to use your money in two directions.

Restating of content and theme: You need to save for retirement and would like a vacation fund . . . and consequently you're frustrated.

In restating the content there is no need to sound like a parrot or a tape recorder. You can change sentence order in such a way that restating does not sound like an echo. For example:

Client: I'm caught between making a real secure investment and taking a few more risks.

Financial professional: You're wondering if you should take a few more risks or stay with a real secure investment.

vs.

Financial professional: You're wondering if you should make a real secure investment or take a few more risks.

In this example there are two equivalent forms of restating of content. The first reverses the order of the client's communication. The second maintains the order. By simply reversing the order you can add variety to restatements.

Restating attempts to communicate back to clients the essence of what they have said. It thereby provides feedback to clients through which they can judge whether they are communicating what they desire. One of the primary purposes of restating is to assess the accuracy of the information exchanged. Restating is analogous to holding up a mirror to the client. A mirror is used to obtain direct feedback when we shave, apply makeup, or comb our hair. Whereas a mirror provides us with visual feedback, a restating response provides a verbal mirror so that you and the client can determine whether you are accomplishing what you want in the communicative process.

Restating is also a way to communicate several qualities considered earlier. Through restating, you can communicate empathy or understanding; acceptance of the client and the problem or issue under discussion; warmth and willingness to engage the client in a personal relationship; and encouragement for further discussion of the problem or issue.

⋙**HELPING THEM HELPS YOU**→ When clients are encouraged to talk more about problems, issues, or goals, they usually add detail. Addition of detail helps you in all aspects of working with your clients.

▶*Paraphrasing*. A second way in which financial professionals can verbally pace is through paraphrasing. Paraphrasing, unlike restating, is the process of taking the essential content of the client communication and restating it in your own words. Examples of paraphrasing are given below.

Client: I think I'm about ready to get involved in a riskier investment.

Financial professional: You feel like it's time to take a few financial chances.

Client: Do you think that I should be considering tax shelters?

Financial professional: You'd like to know if I think you're ready to shelter some of your capital.

Client: I've been thinking about mutual funds as a primary source of investment.

Financial professional: You think that mutual funds can best serve your financial needs.

In each of these examples, the professional has attempted to repeat for the client the essential message the client wishes to communicate. The professional does this in his or her own words. It is important to note that, like restating, each professional paraphrase is essentially equivalent to the client statement and does not add any additional information.

Both restating and paraphrasing provide you a means of sharing your understanding of the client's message. Neither adds new information. Yet both communicate understanding, and consequently they open the interview to further and deeper discussion. A result of the effective use of restating and paraphrasing is development of mutual trust between you and your clients, trust that can lead to more accurate goal definition, better problem resolution, appropriate decision making, and eventually a more effective financial plan.

Obviously, restating and paraphrasing, by themselves, cannot provide total communication. Rather, they serve as a form of verbal pacing. Along with summarizing, the third skill to be discussed below, restating and paraphrasing establish a feedback link between you and your clients. This link is essential to effective professional relationships.

▸ *Summarizing*. Summarizing serves the same general purpose as restating and paraphrasing. It is especially useful when the client has talked for an extended period in an attempt to explain his or her situation. For example:

Client: As you know I'm just getting into this financial planning business . . . I've got a lot of questions . . . I mean . . . I want to use my money wisely . . . I've got a lot of plans for the future. . . .

Financial professional: You're new at this way of planning your financial future and you want to make sure you make wise choices.

In this example, summarizing is used to tie a number of the client's ideas together. This provides the client an opportunity to hear what she has said and an opportunity to correct any miscommunication between herself and the professional. A second use of summarizing is to bring closure to a portion of the client/professional communication and to provide structure for further discussions. As a result of the above interchange the professional could focus discussion on (1) the client's newness to financial planning, (2) the client's need to make wise choices, or (3) the client's plans for her future, or on a combination of these points.

Summarizing is also an important technique to use in bringing a professional session to a close. At the end of the session, it is important to know what has transpired and what, if anything, needs to be accomplished in the near future. For example, consider the situation where the client suggests readiness to make a financial commitment to a real estate purchase but that additional information about its liquidity is needed. If you were the financial professional, you might summarize the financial planning session like this:

Financial professional: We've talked about a number of financial investment possibilities. In looking at a number, corporate bonds, commodities, precious metals, and real estate, you've settled on real estate. But before you make a final decision you'd like me to check out the liquidity factor of this one particular offering.

After obtaining client agreement on the summarized material, you might conclude by saying, "By our next meeting I'll have the information you requested."

Finally, summarizing is a useful process to begin a professional session with a client who has been seen before. Summarizing at the start of a session will provide a review of what has previously transpired and set the stage for the present meeting. As an example, consider the following:

Financial professional: The last time we met we talked about a number of financial possibilities, corporate bonds, commodities, precious metals, and real estate. You settled on real estate, but you asked if I would check out the liquidity factor on one particular offering. I did. Here is the information you requested.

In this summary the same material was addressed as was presented in the earlier closing summary. This approach is one way of tying two sessions together, keeping the focus on the client, and avoiding undue repetition. A second session can begin where the first ended.

Restating, paraphrasing, and summarizing are used by professionals to build a sound relationship. These responses do not add to what a client says but provide a feedback link between the professional and client. This allows the professional to check accuracy of communication and encourages participation.

The verbal pacing skills of restating, paraphrasing, and summarizing are effective skills to help you begin understanding the client's experiential map. You can increase your understanding and communicative power if you also attend to several other elements as the client communicates.

Pacing Learning Styles. Earlier we discussed how people develop their personal experiential maps through use of their senses and how sensory experiences become part of the stored information in our experiential maps. As adults we use three primary information processing modes: visual (images), auditory (sounds), and kinesthetic (feeling or action).

▶ The *visual* learning style usually refers to pictorial representations of events and is characterized by words that embody vision, for example, seeing, picturing, reflecting, and mirroring.

▶ The *auditory* learning style refers to hearing, word characterizations, abstract thinking, and verbal analysis. This learning style is typified by words such as thinking, knowing, analyzing, assessing, evaluating, and appraising.

▶ The *kinesthetic* learning style encompasses feelings and actions and is represented by words like sensing, feeling, and exciting and words like forcing, being, doing, and acting.

As discussed previously, people usually develop a preferential way of processing information, that is, of acquiring, processing, storing, and communicating information. We referred to these preferences as learning styles. In financial relationships it is important to approach clients from their preferred learning styles to build and maintain rapport. The importance of pacing the basic learning style of clients can be understood if we examine common human experiences. For instance, have you ever had an argument or heated discussion with someone only to find out later that you were both saying the same thing? This can happen if one person discusses the topic from one preferred learning style and the second person discusses the topic from another preferred learning style. While both may be sharing the same perspective, it may sound like they have quite different opinions. Frequently, the realization comes later that both were saying essentially the same thing. These kinds of interactions can be avoided in financial situations if professionals make specific attempts to verbally pace their clients' learning style preferences.

While there are formal ways to measure preferred learning styles and preferred information processing modes, there usually is neither the time nor the opportunity in the financial process to do so. The easiest way to gather this information is to listen carefully to the client's use of language. When people speak, you can get a deeper understanding of their experiential map if you listen carefully to their verbs, adjectives, and adverbs. By pacing these kinds of words, you can restate, paraphrase, or summarize while matching the learning styles of your clients. Consider the following client statement:

Client: Well, I guess the issue is to *see* my financial *picture clearly* so that I can *look* toward the future. If I can *focus* on what is necessary for the kids' education, I might be able to *see* what I need to do.

When you examine the verbs, adverbs, and adjectives in the client statement, you will notice that they are mostly visual. When people talk, the verbs, adverbs, and adjectives they use will usually give you an indication of their preferred sensory operation mode or learning style. Verbal pacing, using the techniques of restating, paraphrasing, and summarizing, would suggest that the professional attempt to match the type of verbs, adverbs, and adjectives used by the client.

For example, in response to the client statement above, you could verbally pace by saying, "You want to *focus* on what you *see* as necessary to prepare for your children's education." On the other hand, you could verbally pace the content of the client's statement without pacing the learning style level of the client's perceptual map by saying, "You want to analyze what will be necessary for your children's education." While the second example accurately reflects content, it does not pace the client's verbs, adverbs, or adjectives, and consequently does not match the client's experiential map. Verbal pacing that includes a matching of client verbs, adverbs, and adjectives deepens the client's feelings of acceptance and understanding. This leads to trust that is essential for effective financial planning and action. Other examples of statements that reveal visual representational maps:

I don't *see* how . . .

I try to *watch* out for things that . . .

I'm not *clear* right now. If only I could *focus* on . . .

A client could say the same thing as our previous client but from an auditory learning style:

Client: Well, I guess the issue is to *analyze* my situation enough to *know* what the future might be. If I can *analyze* what is necessary for the kids' education, I might be able to *talk* myself into doing what I need to do.

When you examine this client statement, you will notice that although it says essentially the same thing as the first client statement, the verbs, adverbs, and adjectives all relate to hearing or analyzing. If you respond with visual verbs, adverbs, and adjectives, you might be accurate about the content but would not match the client's preferred way of processing information. Other examples of how auditory representational maps are reflected:

I keep *analyzing the situation but can't find a solution.*

I keep *telling* myself to plan better.

I give myself these pep *talks* all the time about . . .

Again, we can go back to our original client statement to determine what it might sound like if the client's preferred learning style were kinesthetic.

Client: Well, I guess the issue is to *get* myself *straightened out* enough to *plan* for the future. If I can *get a handle on* what is necessary for the kids' education, I might be able to *force* myself into doing what I need to do.

Notice that the client's verbs, adverbs, and adjectives almost all deal with feelings and actions—kinesthetic. You can deepen your level of expressed understanding by matching the verbs, adverbs, and adjectives of the client when you verbally pace through restatement, paraphrasing, or summarizing. Kinesthetic examples from an *emotional* perspective include the following:

▸It's so *depressing* to think about buying life insurance.

▸It's *really exciting* to think about all these possibilities.

▸You know it's *really hard* to keep all the possibilities in mind.

Or from an *action* perspective:

▸Well, it's time I *really got going* with my finances.

▸It's *really hard to keep pushing* myself like this and having inflation *eat* things away.

▸I don't know where *to go* for . . .

Or, finally, from a *sensory* perspective:

▸It's a *bitter* pill *to swallow.*

▸I just *keep getting* this deep *sense* that something may *go* wrong.

▸I *smell* something *fishy* in this deal.

When people talk, their verbs, adverbs, and adjectives paint a picture that provides an understanding of how they experience their worlds. The verbs, adverbs, and adjectives also provide information about how they are processing and storing information in their representational maps. When we verbally pace clients, we communicate to them that we are listening to their general ideas and listening to how they are processing those ideas.

When people feel *stuck* in decision making, they may be simultaneously having experiences in two different representational systems, or having two incompatible experiences. While they may *know* what they need to do, they may not be able to *see* how it will turn out or *feel* comfortable with the ensuing decision. The internal conflict precludes any decision. Consider these statements, for example:

▸I would really like to *get out* of this investment but I can't ever *see* my way *clear*.

▸I *have no idea* what the reason is and I can't ever *see* myself *doing* it.

Two important keys appear in these client statements. First, there are essentially two sentences held together by the words *but* or *and*. Second, when you examine the two sentences in the first example, you will notice that the verbs, adverbs, and adjectives in the two sentence segments are at different sensory levels. For example, *get out* (kinesthetic) and *see/clear* (visual). Sentences such as this convey the client's confusion about an issue. The confusion stems from having two different experiences at the same time—feeling on the one side and seeing on the other.

It is possible to experience two different or conflicting things at the same time if there is a difference between the senses used for each experience: visual and auditory, or visual and kinesthetic, for example. It is very hard to have two opposing experiences at the same time through the same sensory system. That is, it is difficult to visually represent two contradictory objects at the same time or simultaneously experience two opposing feelings. For example, it is highly unlikely that you would be both happy and sad at the same time or that you could simultaneously imagine a peaceful situation and a chaotic one.

When a client has two distinct experiences, through two sensory levels, you can use verbal pacing skills to help the client transpose both experiences—visual and kinesthetic, for example—into one or the other of the systems. This will help the client separate the experiences. The client will experience first one, then the other, but not both at the same time. To do this, you merely employ a good listening response that uses similar verbs, adverbs, and adjectives in both halves of your response rather than using two different sensory systems as the client does. Consider the following example of this idea.

Client: I would really like to *get out* of this investment but I can't ever *see* my way *clear*.

Financial Professional: You would like to *see* yourself out of this investment but you can't *see* your way *clear*.

In this example the professional has transformed the first kinesthetic verb into the visual mode to be consistent with the second half of the sentence. This sorting out process will help the client to relieve the confusion and sense of being stuck. A second alternative is to transform the client verbs, adverbs, or adjectives to the third sensory system, away from the two expressed by the client. For example:

Financial Professional: You *tell* yourself you ought to get rid of that investment but you also *tell* yourself you can't.

In this response the professional has transformed the client's kinesthetic and visual verbs and adverbs into the third mode, auditory. This helps clients to separate their experiences, allowing them to deal with distinct or opposing issues one at a time.

As the previous discussion indicates, effective communicators identify how people experience their worlds by listening intently to their verbs, adverbs, and adjectives and respond to clients in a manner that mirrors how clients express themselves. Below are further examples of how people might express themselves from the various forms of learning styles:

Auditory examples:

- I listen to all of this advice . . .
- I keep telling myself what I ought to do.
- I can talk myself into just about anything.
- I just keep hearing the same advice over and over.
- I wish I had the right words to motivate myself.
- I have trouble hearing what he is trying to say.
- She never listens to me.
- Just tell me what to do.

Notice that in each of the examples the verbs, adjectives, or adverbs all refer to listening or talking. Words of this type are all associated with an auditory learning style.

Visual examples:

- I don't see what you mean.

▶ I can't see my way clear to do that right now.
▶ I wish I could get a clear picture of what to do.
▶ From my view . . .
▶ Everything is so black right now.
▶ Everything is just so fuzzy.
▶ I keep looking for the right answers.
▶ I have this vision of what I want.
▶ I need something to brighten up my life.

Notice that each of these examples expresses something visual. When you read them or listen to someone talking this way, you can usually form a mental picture yourself. In the examples it is clear the person speaking is processing information through some form of mental picture.

The kinesthetic examples which follow are broken into three subcategories—kinesthetic action, kinesthetic emotion, and kinesthetic sensory.

Kinesthetic action examples:

▶ I've got to get going with my plans.
▶ I keep trying but don't seem to get anywhere.
▶ I want to find something that is meaningful.
▶ I keep running around for advice.
▶ That was an uplifting experience.
▶ It's like I'll never get there.
▶ No matter how I try . . .
▶ He drives himself until he drops.

Kinesthetic emotion examples:

▶ I'm so depressed about . . .
▶ I'm about as happy with ——— as I've ever been.
▶ I get so darn mad when . . .
▶ You feel so taken advantage of.
▶ It's just such a sickening feeling.
▶ I guess I can't be happy about ——— all the time.
▶ Do you ever just feel blah about ———?

Kinesthetic sensory examples:

▶ Things just smell fishy about that deal.
▶ That deal smells!
▶ I just get this bad taste in my mouth about ———.
▶ I'll just grit my teeth and choose something.
▶ It's such a bitter pill to swallow.
▶ That deal is so sweet!
▶ She is so sickeningly sweet all the time.

Notice that the verbs, adjectives, and adverbs in the kinesthetic examples all indicate someone who is experiencing a world of action, feeling, taste or smell. Such a person usually experiences the world at a concrete sensory level. Such a person may find it difficult to deal at a more abstract or theorizing level. This type of person frequently asks, "So, what does that mean in practical terms?" Effective communicators, despite their own natural tendencies or learning styles, learn to assess the learning style of clients and respond to clients in the clients' style.

There is a final category called the "Metaphorical-Visual" category. In this category a client's verbs, adjectives, and adverbs may be difficult to classify, and yet, when you listen closely to content, it is fairly obvious that the client is trying to paint a verbal, but metaphorical, picture of personal experience.

Metaphorical-visual examples:

- ▸It's like being caught in a never-ending circle.
- ▸It's like being in a fun house and trying to find the way out.
- ▸I wish I could just find the right path up the mountain.
- ▸I feel like I'm caught on a ferris wheel and can't get off.
- ▸Life is just one big garbage dump right now.
- ▸I guess I've got three strikes against me.
- ▸It's like a knife through hot butter.

Notice in these examples that some of the verbs, adjectives, and adverbs refer to kinesthetic, auditory, or visual experiences. However, the overall effect of the statements is to create a mental picture or metaphor to explain an experience. Such metaphorical language is very rich because it usually contains or activates elements of all three learning styles. You may have noticed that effective speakers usually use metaphorical language as a way of reaching each person in the audience. The same approach works for one-to-one communication.

Pacing Language Levels. As professionals, we often forget that clients do not always have the knowledge or the extensive vocabulary we have about our field. That, of course, is one of the reasons they come to see us. However, that difference in knowledge and vocabulary can become a source for problems. The *jargon* each field develops is a useful tool for communication among professionals. Jargon is a shorthand way of expressing a great number of complicated and detailed concepts. However, when we use such jargon with clients we often forget that they might not know what we are talking about. Simple concepts for you, like *remainderman*, *selling short*, *debit*, and *cash value* may be Greek to the lay person.

When you begin building a professional relationship, you should spend as much time as possible assessing the client's level of understanding and professional vocabulary. This should be done slowly and purposefully. Once you have a sense of the client's sophistication, you can choose vocabulary and concepts that pace the client's present level of knowledge or understanding. A quick way to destroy rapport and trust is to discuss important concepts with vocabulary the client has difficulty comprehending. Following are four examples that examine this attitude. The first two demonstrate nonpacing, the second two, pacing.

Don't:

Client: I don't want to take any risks with my money.

Financial professional: You believe that it is inappropriate to invest your resources in something that has low credibility and high expectation of forfeiture.

Client: I need some financial advice.

Financial professional: You'd like relevant information pertaining to acceptable investment opportunities.

In both of these examples, the professional has moved beyond the client and has used words that, although accurate, do not *pace* the client. The degree of sophistication in your response should match the sophistication level of the client's question or statement. Consider the next examples:

Do:

Client: I believe I'd like to expand my financial base.

Financial professional: You think it's time to enlarge your financial holdings.

Client: I can see that I need a clearer picture of investment opportunities.

Financial professional: I can help you look at some financial possibilities.

In these examples the professional has paced the client on two levels. First, the financial professional paced the content through a content paraphrase. Second, the client's verbs were paced. The word *believe* (auditory) was paced with the word *think* (auditory) and the word *expand* (kinesthetic) was paced with the word *enlarge* (kinesthetic). In a similar manner, the professional paced *see* and *clearer picture* (both visual) with *look at* (visual).

In summary, communication is fostered if you use words similar (in level of sophistication) to the client's and if you pace the client's primary sensory system by attending to his or her verbs, adverbs, and adjectives.

Pacing Tonality, Rate, and Volume. Additional forms of verbal pacing revolve around tonality, rate, and volume. You naturally attend to these elements. When someone raises his or her voice to you, you usually raise your voice. Or, when people whisper to us, we generally tend to lower our voices and whisper. While we do these things almost automatically, one advanced technique is to purposely match (pace) the client's level of communication. We can use this natural process to our advantage. When a client is agitated or angry and we use a calm, slow speech rate in a low tone, the client will generally slow down to meet our level of communication. In other words, the client will have a natural tendency to pace our speech pattern and consequently will start speaking in a slower, calmer manner.

CHAPTER 6

Exploring Skills

Information Gathering. In Chapter 5 we discussed the basic communication skills flowing from the concept of pacing. We now turn our attention to skills that can be used to gather information and explore details of the client's representational map. The normal and useful way of gathering information or exploring is through the use of questions. However, if you continuously use questions, the communicative interaction can take on the characteristics of an interrogation. You need additional ways to gather information and to explore.

One method of exploring was considered in the discussion of verbal pacing. If you recall, verbal pacing skills are used to help you get in touch with the client's representational map, which in turn helps you to establish open, trusting relationships based on understanding the client. A second level of exploration is needed to generate the quantitative and qualitative details relevant to client goals and resources. Without specific details, you are hampered in your efforts to make pertinent recommendations. You can utilize three basic skills to gather information or to explore with clients—Selective Pacing, Imperative Statements, and Questions.

Finally, advanced exploration techniques are needed to help clients clarify the meaning of their statements and to help them become aware of verbal and nonverbal discrepancies. Word clarification and concept clarification are helpful to accomplish the former, whereas the latter can be accomplished if you attend to the client's expressed or implied ambivalences, stated or implied logical inconsistencies, unrealistic goals, areas of implied causation, and generalizations.

Selective Pacing. In selective pacing you can use the verbal pacing skills of restating, paraphrasing, and summarizing to gather information and explore. In Chapter 5 we discussed restatement as a way of building a relationship and providing communicative feedback. We also suggested that restatement could be used to check the accuracy of the communicative interaction. In addition, restatement of a selected portion of the client's statements can be used as a way of exploring one specific aspect of the client communication without having to ask a question. For example, consider the following interaction:

Client: Well, my last kid just graduated from college . . . I'm not getting any younger . . . I guess I'm ready to put a little more into stocks . . . What do you think?

Financial professional (using selective restatement): Let's see . . . you think you're ready to invest a little more in stocks.

Client: Well, yeah. Stocks seem to be doing real well . . . and the money I was using for my kid's education I can now put to work. It seems like a good chance to build up a retirement nest egg.

As you can see from this example, you can explore and gather information without having to resort to questions. In this example the professional elicited additional information from the client by using selective restatement. This form of response allows you to respond to that portion of the client's statement that seems most appropriate. Once aspects of that segment of the client's statement are thoroughly discussed, you can continue the conversation by selectively restating another portion of the client's original statement. For example, from the example above, ''You say this is a good chance to build a nest egg. . . .'' Or you can introduce an entirely different line of inquiry; for example, ''What other forms of investment have you considered?'' The advantage of a selective restatement is that you can use the client's statements to provide the basis for obtaining additional information. This approach adds variety to the interchange, helps you understand the client's representational map, and communicates to the client caring and understanding.

Imperative Statements. The simple imperative sentence can be used by you to clarify meaning, encourage client participation, and obtain additional information. For example:

Client: I think I'd like to start preparing for my retirement.

Financial professional: Tell me about your retirement plans.

The statement ''Tell me . . .'' encourages the client to add information. Other imperative statements include ''Expand on that . . .,'' ''Elaborate on that . . .,'' ''Explore that further . . .,'' ''Give me more detail,'' and so on. Each of these leads places responsibility on the client to provide more detailed information about the topic under discussion. By using selective restatements (verbal pacing) and imperative statements, you can explore and gather a wealth of information without asking questions.

Questions. As you have seen, it is possible to gather information without the use of questions. However, there are times when you will need to ask questions to obtain specific information. The six basic types of questions along with their strengths and weaknesses are discussed below.

▸*Yes/No questions*. Questions of this type usually are asked in such a way that the client can respond with a simple *yes* or *no*. For example, ''Did you bring the information I asked for?'' This question can be answered *yes* or *no*. It does not encourage the client to offer additional information. Because the client is being asked to respond to the question, she may comply exactly, despite the fact that you may really want her to elaborate on the issue being discussed. If a positive relationship has been established with the client, you are more likely to receive additional information even if you ask a yes/no question. Otherwise, you may be forced to ask another question to keep the communication going. If the client continues to respond with one-word answers, you should check to see if you are using too many yes/no questions.

Yes/no questions, although appearing in a question format, may be used to express a statement or belief. For example, ''Don't you think the President's foreign policy is a good one?'' is a disguised statement which says in effect, ''I think the President's foreign policy is a good one.'' When we use this kind of yes/no question/statement, we strongly imply the desired answer. In this example, the speaker wants a *yes* response from the listener. If the listener doesn't give the expected *yes* a disagreement could result. You should be extremely careful in using yes/no question/statements. It is much better to state ideas directly than to imply them through yes/no questions. The yes/no question/statement frequently makes people feel manipulated, which in turn affects trust in the relationship.

Yes/no questions can be an effective tool if you use them purposefully. They can be used to control the type of information and the amount of client talk. For example:

Client: I think that I'm ready for an ongoing investment program.

Financial professional: Are you willing to commit money to this program on a regular basis?

Client: Yes.

Financial professional: Are you willing to invest $100 every month?

Client: Yes.

In this situation the financial professional used two yes/no questions to move the client from generalized thought about entering a regular investment program to a definite commitment of $100 per month for such an investment.

Further, yes/no questions can be used to establish a *yes set*. This use of the yes/no question can be used to influence clients by establishing a pattern in which you ask a series of yes/no questions which do imply a *yes* answer. This develops a *yes set* in the client. You can then make your final point, which is intended to influence the client in a particular direction. For example:

Financial professional: You've said you'd like to prepare for retirement . . . is that right?

Client: Yes.

Financial professional: In our last discussion about this, you indicated that to retire at 55 you'd have to supplement your company pension plan . . . correct?

Client: Yes.

Financial professional: Well, since you're 43 now, don't you think that you'd better put money aside on a monthly basis to meet your goal?

Client: Yes.

This use of the yes/no question has several dangers. The first, of course, is that the client may feel manipulated and then may resist all efforts at influence. While this *yes* set use of the yes/no question may be very powerful, it can sound like a typical sales pitch, which in turn may turn the client away. If used judicially, the *yes set* pattern of the yes/no questions can be a powerful tool in your arsenal of communicative skills.

▶ *Multiple choice questions*. This form of question usually provides the client with a number of alternative choices. For example:

Financial professional: What sort of real estate are you interested in? Commercial? Houses? Apartments?

The usual motivation in asking a multiple choice question is to help the client talk more about the topic at hand. Again, even though multiple choice questions can lead to open exploration by the client once trust is built, they present dangers similar to those inherent in using yes/no questions. That is, the client simply has to choose one of the alternatives to respond to the question. There are certainly times when you want to limit the client's response to a choice of one of a number of possibilities. However, if you want open exploration on the client's part, then the use of multiple choice questions may produce the opposite effect.

There are also situations in which speakers use multiple choice questions to make a statement. This is usually done in an attempt to convince someone to take a specific action. You can lay out a number of alternatives with a multiple choice question and imply which one the client is to choose. This can be done in two ways. You can imply the *correct* response by making several of the alternatives ridiculous or by emphasizing one with your voice. For example:

Financial professional: Well, what do you want to do, just leave your money in a regular bank account and let inflation take care of most of it, or invest in something which will really beat inflation?

Client: Well, of course I want to stay ahead of inflation.

The danger with this approach is that the client may feel belittled or manipulated. Although there might be rare occasions when this may be appropriate, you should remember that one of the characteristics of an effective communicative relationship is openness, respect, and honesty. If you honestly believe the client should do what he or she has in mind, it is better to state it directly, and not imply the answer through multiple choice questions.

▸*Dilemma questions*. A dilemma question is asked in such a way that two alternatives are posed so that (1) no matter how clients respond they may be wrong, or (2) neither alternative is what clients really want. For example, the old comedian's line "Have you stopped beating your wife?" cannot be answered without the husband incriminating himself. If a man answers "yes," it means he has been beating his wife; and if he answers "no," it means that he still is beating his wife. Usually, this form of question is inappropriate in professional relationships. Dilemma questions, like multiple choice questions, can have the effect of making the client feel manipulated and belittled.

It should be noted, however, that the second form of the dilemma question, giving the client a choice between two alternatives, neither of which he or she really wants, is frequently used. For example, at the doctor's office the nurse may ask you, "Do you want your shot in the arm or in the fanny?" The nurse has assumed that you would prefer to get your medicine through a shot rather than through a pill or liquid. Her dilemma question prevents you from alternative choices. A financial example of this form of the dilemma question might be, "Would you like to make your monthly investments through a checking account draft or by mailing them in directly?"

While there are dangers to the dilemma question in that the client may feel manipulated or belittled, there are times when you might use the second form of the dilemma question to help clients move toward needed decisions. This second form of the *dilemma* question can be used effectively to reduce resistance and will be discussed further in Chapter 7.

▸*Level I probe questions*. Level I probe questions are used to gather factual information that is verifiable in some way. For example, demographic data such as name, address, telephone number, and place of work can be asked with Level I probe questions. Level I probe questions usually follow the normal interrogatives of *who, what, when, where, how*, and sometimes *why*. Demographic data is usually gathered easily and efficiently by using client information forms before planninng sessions begin. However, some information necessary for planning can be gathered during interviews. For example, consider the following:

Financial professional: How long have you been employed by your present employer?

Client: Four years.

Financial professional: Hmm . . . What type of retirement plan is provided by your company?

Client: A complete package . . . I mean . . . I can retire at 62 or with 30 years of service, whichever comes first, at 66% of my final base salary.

Financial professional: I see . . . that sounds quite good. When do you think you'll retire?

Client: I haven't figured out the exact year, but I know I'll be 62!

Financial professional: You sound very certain about how old you'll be . . . what would you like to have built up in securities by then?

. . . And so on.

Probes of the type used in this example are most effective when used in combination with the Level II probes discussed below.

▸*Level II probe questions*. Level II probe questions are very similar in form to Level I probe questions. That is, they usually use the interrogatives *who, what, how, when, where*, and sometimes *why*. The difference lies in the kind of information you are attempting to acquire. While Level I probe questions get at factual information, Level II probe questions usually attempt to get the client's deeper response or feelings about the information being discussed. For example:

Level I probe question: What kind of insurance would you like to purchase?

Level II probe question: What is there about that type of insurance that makes you think it will meet your needs?

As you will notice, the Level II probe question attempts to get at information concerning the client's underlying feelings about a type of insurance. While Level I probe questions provide necessary information for the beginning of planning, Level II probe questions provide information that is necessary to develop effective proposals for the client. Level II probe questions solicit details about the client's representational map which form the basis for choosing one alternative over others. There may be a number of equally good proposals for the client. You may need to understand deeper aspects of the client's map to help the client make decisions or to choose among the various alternatives.

Both Level I and Level II probe questions follow the normal interrogatives *who, what, when, where, how*, and sometimes *why*. *Why* is listed as "sometimes" because *why* questions solicit some degree of defensiveness. Throughout our lives, parents, teachers, and other authorities have asked *why* questions when they wanted us to explain ourselves. For example, "Why didn't you clean your room?" or "Why didn't you get your homework done?" When you heard such questions, you usually began to fear a little and intuitively knew that no excuses would be accepted. Of course, the tone of voice with which *why* questions are asked will have a great effect upon the message conveyed. Regardless of the tone of voice, *why* questions tend to make people defensive.

►*The faulty question.* Faulty questions follow the normal Level I or Level II probe/question format, but if you analyze them, you will find them to be logically inappropriate. For example, a young lad comes home in the winter without his mittens and Dad asks, "Where did you lose them?" On the surface this sounds like a normal question. However, when examined, the question appears to be inappropriate. If the lad knew where he lost the mittens, he would have found them and brought them home. The usual answer from the boy is, "I don't know." At this point Dad might follow with another faulty question: "Why don't you know?" This second question asks the boy to make some statement about how he knows and remembers. If the boy knew the answer to this question, he wouldn't have lost his mittens in the first place. At this time the boy can only make one appropriate answer, "You see, Dad, as a human I have short-term memory and long-term memory. Where I set my mittens down must have gone into short-term memory, and since it has been longer than five minutes, I no longer remember." You can imagine what kind of response that would elicit from Dad!

In professional financial relationships there are also examples of faulty questions. "Why didn't you sell that stock when you saw that it was dropping so fast?" There are only two possible answers: "I thought it would go back up," and "If I had known it would drop that far, I would have sold it." The major point to be made is that if you ask questions, make sure they are questions that help clients explore further or that add pertinent information.

Advanced Exploration Techniques. When people talk, they assume that other people understand exactly what they are saying. That is, they assume that other people mean the same thing with any word or phrase that they do. As discussed earlier, the words we use are an attempt to express some part of our experiential map. The same word or phrase will not mean the same thing to each individual. What makes this condition even more difficult is that some words are more expressive than others (expressive in the sense of being open to many possible interpretations), while other words or phrases would be accepted unilaterally.

Word/Concept Clarification. The kinds of words we use to describe our experiences vary on a continuum from concrete to abstract. Concrete words have few possible interpretations, while abstract words have many possible interpretations. For example, when you hear the word *dog*, you intuitively know that the word does not refer to any particular dog or, sometimes, that the word may not even refer to an animal. While it may refer to a mutt, a collie, or a Great Dane, it may also refer to an object, an ugly person, a slow car, and so on. The word *dog* lacks a *referential index*. It doesn't refer to anything specifically. You may have experienced the lack of referential index in listening to politicians. They can talk for a long time, sound wonderful, but say very little. A financial example may illustrate this concept.

Client: Well, you know how it is. It's awfully hard to keep track of my investments.

While it appears that the client statement is understandable, it is filled with abstract words and has very little referential index.

▸*You*. The pronoun may refer to the client, it may refer to a generalized group of people as with the word everyone, or it may refer to the financial professional.

▸*It/It's*. Refers to something, but what specifically is unclear.

▸*To keep track*. Does this mean to know, to count, to be aware of, to watch, to follow, or something else? Each verb phrase, when substituted for the original in the client statement, changes the meaning slightly but importantly.

►*Investments*. What investments are being referred to is unclear at this point. Is the client referring to savings accounts, stocks, bonds, direct participation programs, real estate? Again, when investments are defined specifically, the client statement takes on a different meaning.

Although the client statement appears to have meaning, when the words are examined it becomes clear that there is much more that needs to be known before we can understand fully what the client is trying to express.

On an emotional level, it is quite evident that the client is frustrated about his investments. Intuitively, the professional might respond to the client's rate of speech, tonality, speech volume, and nonverbal clues. All of these clues, plus the context in which clients make statements, provide a basis for knowing what the client is saying, despite the use of abstract words and lack of referential index.

Another example may clarify this concept. A parent might hear a child say, "Mary hurt Johnny!" Immediately this announcement makes sense. An immediate intuitive reaction might be, "Is he hurt badly?" The usual secondary reaction is, "How did she hurt him?" Our intuition tells us that we really don't know how *hurt* is being used. Mary could have hurt Johnny by hitting him, pushing him, hugging him, or some other act, and *hurt* could mean physical or even emotional hurt. We intuitively know to ask for more specific information so that we can respond appropriately to the situation.

In a similar way, there are times in professional relationships when seeking such specific information is extremely important. For instance, if a client stated, "I think that what I'm paying for insurance is way out of line, and further it's just costing too much," you probably would respond intuitively to a number of elements in the client's statement. First, you might wonder what insurance? The car insurance? Life insurance? Homeowner's insurance? All of these? Second, you might question the phrase "way out of line." You might be curious about the client's reference point; "way out of line" as compared to what? Compared to another insurance company's rates? Compared to a friend's insurance rates? The reference point needs to be defined to know what the client means. Third, the statement "It's just costing too much" would probably lead you to wonder how much it actually costs; what "just costing too much" is being compared to; or whether the statement "just costing too much" is appropriate at the present moment but not in the past, or possibly, in the future. All of these intuitive responses are natural and appropriate. Answers to them would help you to understand your client's representational map and help in the total professional relationship.

In a similar manner, you can foster the professional process if you (1) become attuned to the words clients use, words such as investments, stock, money, expenditures, assets, and liabilities, and (2) use your awareness to clarify words that are vague or unclear. For instance, look at the following client statements as examples that illustrate these points.

▸I think my investments are quite sound, my cash reserves are good and my income is steady.

▸My stocks are not doing very well in today's market and I'm starting to worry about what I should do.

▸I've got my money tied up in limited partnerships.

▸My expenditures are just too high.

▸I can use my assets as collateral.

▸My liabilities are out of proportion.

Selective restatement of vague words or phrases like those in the six client statements above will usually elicit further discussion, elaboration, and clarification. Imperative statements can also be used to help clients be more specific about their needs and wants. Finally, of course, questions about what the client specifically means can also be used. The following interchanges exemplify how you can clarify client words or concepts.

Client: I think my investments are quite sound, my cash reserves are good, and my income is steady.

Financial professional (using a selective restatement): You say your investments are quite sound.

⋙**USE SILENCE**→ If you emphasize the word *investments* in the selective restatement and then wait quietly, the client probably will expand on what investments she is thinking about. Word emphasis plus silence is the key in this approach.

Client: My stocks are not doing very well in today's market and I'm starting to worry about what I should do.

Financial professional (using a selective restatement): You say your stocks are not doing very well.

> ⋙**WHAT TO EMPHASIZE**→ Voice emphasis on the word *stocks* and possibly on the words *doing very well* coupled with appropriate silence can foster client exploration.

Client: I've got my money tied up in limited partnerships.

Financial professional (Using an imperative statement): Tell me specifically which money you've got tied up.

Client: My expenditures are just too high.

Financial professional (using an imperative statement): You say that your expenditures are too high . . . tell me which expenditures you are referring to.

> ⋙**IMPERATIVE RESPONSE**→ In the client statements above, the words *money* and *expenditures*, respectively, were vague and lacked specificity. Imperative leads would help the clients to state exactly what they had in mind.

Client: I can use my assets as collateral.

Financial professional (Using a questioning response): Which assets are you referring to?

Client: My liabilities are out of proportion.

Financial professional (Using a questioning response): You say that your liabilities are out of proportion . . . which liabilities . . . specifically . . . are you thinking about?

or

You say that your liabilities are out of proportion . . . I'm curious . . . out of proportion as compared to what?

In summary, it is important that you utilize a variety of responses. It is through this variety that you can control interviews and help clients to explore more deeply their experiential maps.

Failure to use a variety can result in a less powerful and productive interchange between you and your client. A variety of responses will keep the client somewhat off guard, make you less predictable, provide stimulation for client thought, and generate the specificity needed for helpful professional planning.

Verbal and Nonverbal Discrepancies. In addition to the information gathering techniques discussed above, financial professionals must be able to help clients explore discrepancies in statements and behaviors. These discrepancies are not intentional but can cause clients difficulty in decision-making. Discrepancies usually occur when clients have two opposing feelings, when they are unable to openly accept opposing feelings or responsibilities appropriate to a situation, or when they want to achieve conflicting goals.

Expressed or implied ambivalence. There are times when clients will express conflicting emotions or thoughts about a situation or event. This can be done directly or be implied through nonverbal behavior which is inconsistent with words the client uses.

▶ *Expressed ambivalence*:

Client: I'd like to invest more, but life is so short I want to enjoy it now.

Financial professional: On the one hand you'd like to invest . . . but . . . on the other hand you want to enjoy it now . . . it's confusing to want two things at the same time.

▶ *Implied ambivalence*:

Client (said defensively): I'm going to spend my extra money for a vacation.

Financial professional: You say that you're going to spend the money on a vacation but somehow you don't sound sure that's what you want to do.

Stated or implied logical inconsistencies. At times clients talk about their situation, their problems, or possible solutions without realizing that their statements are inconsistent.

▶ *Stated inconsistency*:

Client: We do budget every month but . . . at the end of the month we just don't know where our money went.

Financial professional: You say that you budget yourselves and yet you don't know where your money goes.

▶ *Implied inconsistency*:

Client: I guess playing the stock market is okay . . . we have to make our money work somehow.

Financial professional: It sounds as though you're not sure that the stock market is a sound way to invest your money.

Unrealistic goals. At times a client's goals, when perceived by another, seem unrealistic. However, *in the client's mind*, the problem is in the situation, not in the perception of the situation.

Client: I'd like for us to invest $500 a month . . . I know that may seem like a lot . . . but if we just cut down on eating out and a little recreation . . . I know we can do it.

Financial professional: I wonder how realistic it is to think that you'll be able to give up such a sizeable portion of your entertainment and budget yourself so tightly.

Implied causation. In this form of discrepancy, clients imply that they have little or no control over an event or situation. This form of discrepancy is characterized by the word *but*. By implication, content that follows the word *but* explains what was said in the first part of the sentence. For example:

Client: I would like to purchase more life insurance *but* I'm buying a new condo.

In this statement the second part of the sentence is used to explain the first part. The client is saying, in effect, that buying a condo is preventing him from buying more life insurance, and by implication, that there is no plausible alternative. Clients will frequently discuss issues in this manner. They may not realize that the implied causation does not prevent them from doing what they state they want, but that the decision they make does. Financial professionals can help clients overcome this situation by helping clients to clarify and understand exactly what they have said. Consider the following responses to the client's statement above:

▸*Question response*:

Financial professional: How does buying a new condo prevent you from purchasing life insurance?

▸*Imperative response*:

Financial professional: Tell me how buying a new condo prevents you from purchasing life insurance.

▸*Restatement*:

Financial professional: You'd *like to* invest in more life insurance *but* buying a new condo is preventing you.

(Emphasis, by the financial professional, is on the words *like to* and *but*.)

You must listen closely to the client's response to any of your statements. The client's explanation may indeed indicate a true causative relationship which prevents him or her from accomplishing a stated goal. On other occasions, you may determine that the major obstacle to client success is the client's financial attitude. For example:

Client: I would like to save more money *but* something always comes up.

Financial professional: Something always comes up to prevent you from saving.

Client: Yeah! . . . Well, you know how it is . . . I just keep seeing things that I'd really like . . . and I have to buy them . . . and I end up not saving.

Financial professional: Why do you say that you *have* to buy them?

Client: Well, I guess I don't *have* to."

Financial professional: I see . . . Tell me more about what you believe to be your long-term financial goals.

In the sequence presented above, the financial professional's primary purpose was to help the client clarify what he wanted or desired. To do this, the financial professional focused on the client's statements and through restatement, questioning, and imperative leads helped the client see more clearly how statements were consistent or inconsistent with stated financial goals.

Generalizations. The natural way of dealing with the world is to put elements we experience into categories or to generalize. We generalize our experiences so that we can make predictions about future events or possibilities. For example, the generalization "*hot stoves burn*" is a useful way of categorizing our experience to prevent burning ourselves in the future. While this process is useful, it can also cause problems. Generalizations can be limiting. Racial or prejudicial statements about social subgroups are limiting. The generalization "*women are terrible drivers*" leads one to believe that all women are bad drivers and fails to allow for the possibility that any woman can be a good driver. Generalizations lack detail which can help individuals respond differentially to unique situations. Thus, the individual who believes that all women are bad drivers is limited to experiencing only women who are bad drivers or making such judgments despite contrary experiences. When meeting a good woman driver, he will ignore her or use her as the exception which proves the rule.

Generalizations lack detail and thus limit the freedom of choice clients have relative to their concerns or goals. You can help clients explore their generalizations, thereby helping them add detail to their experiential maps. In this way you can help your clients increase the number of options available.

Let us examine how generalizations limit freedom of choice. Suppose that the first chair a little boy climbs into happens to be a broken rocking chair. When he climbs into the chair, it tips over, and he falls and hurts his head. In this situation the child can learn that chairs are dangerous; they will tip over; and he will hurt himself. As a result of this generalization, the child limits his potential freedom. He may hesitate to sit in any chair, thus limiting his options to sitting on sofas or the floor.

However, the child might learn a different generalization—rocking chairs are dangerous. In this generalization the child has more freedom. He can now choose to sit on sofas, the floor, and on four-legged, nonrocking chairs. The child could also learn that broken rocking chairs are dangerous. With this generalization the child is left with even more options. He can sit on sofas, on the floor, on four-legged chairs, and on rocking chairs which do not have broken rockers.

As can be seen, generalizations can have a limiting or freeing effect upon choice and eventual behavior. Many times, clients will talk about themselves and their concerns in generalizations that are extremely limiting. It is important in financial situations to help clients recognize how their generalizations limit their freedom of choice.

Generalizations are easily recognizable. They usually contain some word which indicates a universal element, such as *everyone, nobody, people, the guys, the gals, society, everybody, all*, etc. There are also a number of adverbs that indicate generalizations: *always, never, sometimes*, etc.

There are three basic ways you can help clients to explore generalizations: restating the content while emphasizing the generalization; asking the client for an exception to the generalization; and providing the client with an example that would be an exception to the generalization. These approaches are examined through the following examples:

▸*Restatement with emphasis*:

Client: I can't think of any situation in which life insurance would be helpful.

Financial professional: You can't think of *any* situation in which life insurance would be helpful.

▸*Asking for an exception:*

Client: I'd never buy an apartment building.

Financial professional: Can you think of any situation in which such a purchase would benefit you?

▸*Providing an exception:*

Client: Whole life insurance is always a bad purchase.

Financial professional: I can understand your concern . . . yet . . . whole life insurance has a premium that won't increase.

Responding to generalizations is important. By responding, you help clients to add detail to their personal mapping structure, which in turn increases their freedom of choice. One aspect of professional encounters is to organize the amount of detail and information clients have to work with. This increases clients' options and helps them to achieve their financial goals.

CHAPTER 7

Going a Step Further: Advanced Techniques

In the previous chapters we outlined basic principles of communication, communication skills (verbal and nonverbal pacing), and exploring techniques. In this chapter we discuss impediments to good communication, methods for dealing with client resistance, and advanced motivational techniques.

Impediments to Good Communication. In earlier chapters a foundation for good communicative relationships with clients was laid. While we have emphasized principles, positive concepts, skills, and techniques, there are some communicative processes which should be avoided.

Overlong Statements. Statements that are too long often sound like lectures! There are times when you will need to give clients additional information or to correct inaccurate information. However, the most effective professional process is a collaborative problem-solving approach which assumes that both parties are involved and responsible. If you use overlong statements that sound like lectures, there is the danger that you may begin to sound like a parent. Clients may feel belittled or feel that they are being treated like children. As soon as clients begin to feel this way, you may damage the openness and trust necessary for effective financial communication. For example, consider the following:

Client: I think that I'm ready to have a will drawn up.

Professional: I was wondering when you were going to get around to that. You know, it's not so bad . . . I mean . . . having a will doesn't mean you're going to die . . . a person in your situation should probably have considered this long ago . . . and also . . . (continues to talk about the benefits of a will).

Put-Down Questions. We have discussed this kind of question previously under the faulty question section. This type of question is often a rhetorical question, usually spoken with strong emotional overtones of sarcasm, anger, or frustration. For example, a banker asking "Why don't you ever pay more attention to your cash flow?" probably isn't expecting an answer. Rather, the banker is making an emotional statement. A common result of this type of question is that clients will feel defensive and try to justify themselves. While there may be rare occasions when it is appropriate to put clients on the defensive, it is not a good idea to do so by indirectly expressing your emotions through put-down questions. When you are feeling frustrated or angry with clients, you will be more effective by stating your emotions directly. For example, "I get frustrated when you make me entirely responsible for your financial decisions. I wish you would get more involved!" In a congruent manner, this feedback statement tells the client how you feel and points out what you would like. This type of statement, because of its directness and specificity, will raise less client defensiveness than a put-down question.

Speaking in Generalizations. People try to influence one another through generalizations. Most of us have tried this communicative strategy at one time or another. For example, as a teenager, you may have asked to use the family car and received a definite "no" from your parents. Your response might have been something like, "Why not? Everybody else does!" This kind of statement was probably a strong attempt to convince your parents that they should let you use the car. This sort of generalization *implies* that if they were good parents, they would be like everyone else and let you use the car. The usual parental response to this sort of plea is, "Well, we aren't everybody else!" This exemplifies the fact that people usually are aware when others try to manipulate them through the use of generalizations. Consequently, you are advised to be aware of your own use of generalizations.

The use of generalizations in professional interactions usually is subtle. Statements like, "Well, everyone seems to think this investment is sound" and "Most tax accountants are recommending . . ." exemplify this point. These two statements imply that the client should accept what is being recommended because *everyone else* or *most tax accountants* have made similar decisions. A more open and direct approach would be for you to share with the client the characteristics, advantages, and disadvantages of the particular investment technique or tax strategy.

There is a second form of generalization which is equally destructive to effective relationships—the overgeneralization. Overgeneralizations are usually emotional statements that are meant to put someone down. An example of an overgeneralization is, "A simple savings account is never a good way to invest your money!" As with most generalizations, there are usually exceptions which depend upon the attitudes and goals of the client. Words like *never, always, everybody, all,* and *nobody* usually mean that an overgeneralization has been used. In summary, it is better to state your feelings and thoughts directly and congruently than to use generalizations or overgeneralizations.

Mind-Reading Statements. Statements implying that you know what clients are thinking are called mind-reading statements. Examples of mind-reading are: "You don't listen to what I try to tell you" or "You don't care what happens to your money." An alternative to using mind reading is to remember that clients carry out what is best for them, given the information they have in their representational maps (See Principle 1.9). When you make mind-reading statements, you imply that clients are wrong and shouldn't be thinking the way they are. In using feedback, you should label behavior that clients exhibit and state your reactions directly. For example, "You don't act as if your money is important to you and I don't know what to do to help you." This approach is direct and provides clients with specific information about your reactions to their behavior.

"You Did . . ." Statements. The opposite of this statement—"You Didn't . . ."—is also used. These kinds of statements are often used to blame others for their behavior. An example of this type of statement is, "You didn't send me the information you promised!" In this statement, it is obvious that blame is being placed on the recipient of the message, maybe in a highly emotional fashion. Statements like this can do serious damage to an effective professional/client relationship because they indicate that you were right and they were wrong. For instance, you may wish to tell clients, "I told you so!" when they fail to follow financial proposals that would have proven more beneficial than the actions they did take. Even though it may be tempting to do so, it is better to avoid using such statements. A more effective approach is to tell clients what you are thinking or feeling. When you tell clients

directly, you model the openness and honesty you wish to develop in an effective working relationship.

"You Should . . ." Statements. Because one of the major aspects of professional interactions is recommendation of plans, options, and possibilities, *should* statements might appear to be quite appropriate. However, there are two dangers in using *should* statements. First, clients may become defensive because of a history of experiences with people telling them that they *should.* This history can help create elements in clients' representational maps which will lead them to automatically respond defensively whenever someone tells them they *should.* The second danger is that when you use a *should* statement you are making a definite, conclusive statement about what a client ought to do. While this is sometimes appropriate, there is always the danger of suggesting through a *should* statement a course which later proves disastrous. It is usually better to indicate several options to clients and have them choose one. In this way clients make the choice and must accept responsibility for outcomes.

The one exception to these warnings is telling clients what they should do based on sound financial principles. For example, "You should have sufficient cash reserves before you begin speculating in the stock market" or "You should protect yourself with liability insurance rather than taking a chance that nothing will ever happen." *Should* statements of this sort revolve around accepted financial principles and help clients to expand their representational maps so that they can make sound decisions in the future.

Defending Statements. Defending statements are often used to pull rank. In everyday communication they might take a form like "I have a right to talk any way I want" or "Because I'm your father, that's why!" This type of statement usually implies that the listener has no right to question the speaker's behavior, statements, or motivations. In professional interactions, statements of this kind can be blatant ("I was only suggesting that plan for your own good!") or subtle ("I was trying to suggest a plan that seemed to fit the goals we outlined!"). While both statements may be absolutely true, statements of this type will make you sound defensive.

Remember that communicative interactions are reciprocal. What you do or say will affect how clients respond and *vice versa.* In the professional process, defending statements may lead to arguments and may leave both you and your client feeling as if nothing has been settled. It is better to use a direct feedback statement that relates a client's behavior with the consequences being experienced. For example, a client who has persisted in playing the stock market might be told, "I can see the attraction of your investments, but last year you had a net loss of 5% on your ventures . . . this seems to be out of line with your goals to earn a minimum of 10% a year on your money." When clients experience the consequences of their actions, they usually are open to change. By avoiding the use of defending statements, you can help clients to face up to the results of their behavior and, consequently, to make better decisions.

Threatening Statements. Threatening statements call for action. For instance, if you tell someone, "If you say that again, I'm leaving," and they say it again, you are faced with a choice—to leave or to ignore the threatening statement. In either case the ensuing action will be detrimental to the relationship and continuing effective communication. In professional relationships threatening statements are more subtle and frequently take the form of veiled warnings. For example, "If you continue the way you are now, you're going to lose your investments!" While it is appropriate to warn clients about possible consequences of their behavior or decisions, it is not appropriate to use threatening statements to control or manipulate clients. Clients intuitively will know when you are trying to manipulate them and will become defensive. A break in the relationship can be the result.

>>>**HAZARDOUS TO YOUR COMMUNICATION** → All of the following are impediments to good communication: overlong statements, put down questions, generalizations, mind-reading statements, you *did* something statements, you *should* statements, and threatening statements. You should monitor your communication to keep these types of statements to a minimum. To the degree that you accomplish this end, you will be able to establish trouble-free relationships with clients.

Dealing with Resistance. Resistance can be viewed in two different ways. In the first, a person doesn't do what another wishes and resists any attempts to make him or her change. Resistance is also displayed by people who seem to be *closed* in the sense of appearing not to be aware of new information. The statement "Don't confuse me with the facts, my mind is already made up" exemplifies this form of resistance. If you recognize either of these forms of resistance in your clients, keep the following in mind.

Clients are doing the best they can using the stored information they have (see Principle 1.9). If we accept this principle, then we can say that clients are not being resistant but rather that they do not have the information in their representational maps to act differently.

The practical meaning of communication is the response you receive (see Principle 3.5). This principle implies that what we often perceive to be resistance is, in essence, our own inability to communicate in ways that move the client in the direction we think best.

Acceptance of these principles can lead us to the conclusion that there may not be client resistance. Rather, we might conclude that there are clients with limited representational maps and times when we, as financial professionals, are limited in the number and type of responses we can make in a given situation. Given these conclusions, your task is to help clients to integrate new information into their representational maps and to use a wide variety of communicative procedures to assure client acceptance of ideas, suggestions, and information. The following techniques should prove helpful in overcoming resistance from either source:

Using Tentative Qualifiers. In general, people have a tendency to resist *absolute statements*. Absolute statements do not take into account the fact that clients have idiosyncratic representational maps and that their representational maps are accurate for them at the moment. In addition, each of us has a stubborn streak. We automatically resist direct commands when someone tells us how to behave or think in some situations. For example, if someone tells you in a loud, commanding voice to blink your eyes, your usual response is not to blink, or maybe even to open your eyes wider. Clients will most often resist direct commands about their behavior or ways of thinking.

The first set of communication skills to reduce resistance revolves around statements, suggestions, or advice given in tentative ways. This can be done through addition of adverbial qualifiers to the things we say. Words like *usually, sometimes, often, whenever, might, maybe, probably* can be used to soften communication to clients. For example, if instead of an absolute command to blink your eyes, you hear "Sometime in the next few seconds you might blink your eyes," you're more apt to cooperate. The qualifier *might* takes away the command nature of the direction. The qualifier also makes the statement consistent with our subconscious knowledge—that every few seconds we do blink our eyes—and makes the statement something that we will comply with. As an example of this concept, consider the following client/attorney interchanges and the attorney's use of tentative qualifiers.

Client: I don't want to think about having a will drawn up.

Attorney: I can see that discussing this is difficult for you . . . you *might* be ready to discuss the advantages the next time we get together.

Client: I'm not sure my heirs can manage what I want to leave to them.

Attorney: I can understand your concern . . . yet, you'll *probably* find some way to get more specific information about their ability in that area.

Tentative qualifiers allow you to make suggestions in a manner that does not put clients on the defensive. Your idea can be communicated and resistance can be held to a minimum.

Using Dilemma Questions. Another set of communication skills that can be applied to reduce resistance revolves around dilemma questions. If you recall, dilemma questions appear to give clients a choice. When examined, however, the ultimate choice of accepting alternatives or of making any choice at all has been excluded.

Dilemma questions and tentative qualifiers can be combined to make suggestions, give directions, and minimize resistance. For example, "Would you like to make a decision about investing in this real estate venture this week or maybe next week?" When this question is examined, it becomes obvious that the client has not been given a choice of whether to invest but, rather, when she will invest. The addition of *maybe* in the second part of the question also increases the possibility that the client will make a choice. The following are other examples of dilemma questions a financial professional may pose:

- "Would you like to invest $50, $100, or $200 a month in mutual funds?"
- "Would you like to have a will drawn up this week or maybe wait until next week?"
- "Would you like to start a gifting program now or wait until after January 1st?"
- "Would you like to recommend my services to a colleague, or possibly just bring him with you to our next meeting?"

In all of the above, the client is being faced with a dilemma. A choice of either alternative in each question results in a decision to do *something*. In these questions, clients are *not* given the option of doing nothing.

Using Psychology. Communication skills that employ psychology can be used to reduce client resistance. In popular language when someone accuses others of "using psychology on me," the message usually being transmitted is that they are using psychology "to make me do what they want me to do." A famous psychiatrist, Milton H. Erickson, says he first learned about this way of dealing with resistance as he was watching his father trying to get a cow to go into the barn. His father was pulling on a rope attached to the cow's halter as hard as he could while the cow was pulling just as hard in the opposite direction. Erickson reports that he doesn't know why it occurred to him, but he ran over and grabbed the cow's tail and jerked as hard as he could. The cow bolted into the barn. In order to *resist* the new pull on its tail the cow had to move forward into the barn.

In financial encounters we can accomplish a similar thing by using a special linguistic form called *not doing* or *not knowing*. For example, a statement like "You know you *don't* have to talk about anything you don't want to . . ." gives the client permission to avoid what he may not want to share with you. On the other hand, this statement could encourage the client to think about all the concerns he does not want to share with you, and, because the client has been given the responsibility for sharing, actually could lead the client to be more open about all his concerns. Consider the following professional statements as examples of this concept:

- "You don't have to plan for every possible financial contingency."
- "You don't have to think about retirement until you have your kids through college."
- "Obviously, you've thought about how you'd like to distribute your estate."

All of these examples demonstrate the "use of psychology" to encourage clients to think or act. This approach, although effective, should be used carefully and probably should be limited to those cases where *strong* resistance is encountered.

Logical Connections. Finally, awareness of logical connections can be used to overcome resistance. Two thoughts or ideas tied together with logical verbal connectors like *and, when,* and *as* characterize logical connections. For example, "*When* you are doing your monthly budget, you *might* think of ways you can cut corners or to find the needed resources to meet your goals." In this example, two ideas are tied together through the use of the word *when*—doing a budget and finding additional resources. Also notice that the use of a tentative qualifier in the second half of the sentence reduces the possibility of resistance. When using logical connections, it is not necessary for the two ideas, suggestions, or directions to be *logically* consistent. For example, "*When* you are working this week, you might think of other financial objectives that are important to you." In this statement there is no logical connection between working and thinking about financial objectives. However, when clients hear such a statement, it will *seem* to make sense. The suggestion will be subconsciously attended to and help clients, consciously and subconsciously, to think about their financial objectives.

Advanced Motivational Techniques. We now move to advanced techniques that can be used to help clients make decisions and, in the long run, to accomplish their goals. These techniques build on your natural interpersonal inclinations and, in some cases, appear to be doing what comes naturally. However, when used in financial situations, these techniques should be purposeful and controlled.

Using Truisms. A truism is a statement which relates to normal experience and is stated in such a way that when clients hear it, their usual response is, "Oh yeah!" Truisms tap into clients' representational maps in such a way that they recognize the experience, or at least, realize that the truism is something they could have experienced. Consider the following examples of truisms.

- "You say you can't solve this problem, yet, you've solved more complicated ones in the past."
- "You say that right now you're financially pinched, sort of like you've said you were when you first started out."
- (Said to a client who just purchased a new house) "It probably will be like when you purchased your last house . . . somewhat difficult at first, but then it will become continuously easier to make payments."

Notice that with these truisms, statements are used that will encourage clients to examine their previous history as a means for generating ideas or as a source of motivation for dealing with present situations.

Using Generic Examples. Generic examples, like truisms, are drawn from normal life experiences. The reason for using generic examples is to help clients tap into their own representational maps to understand the point, advice, or information being presented. By using the client's own experience you increase the likelihood that the point, advice, or information being offered will be both understood and accepted. For example, in talking to a client about investing in the stock market, you might say something similar to the following:

> "It's like going to a horse race, there are some long shots, and a number of favorites. Also, there are no guarantees—a favorite can lose. On the other hand, even a long shot can pay off."
>
> "It's like investing in society: it will have its ups and

downs, but, if history is any indicator, in the long run, it will be more up than down . . ."

"Involving yourself in the stock market is like marriage . . . the more you invest yourself in the process . . . and the more you work at understanding the intricacies . . . the more likely you are to be successful . . ."

Generic examples can take the form of analogies, like the three above, or of personal examples like the following:

- "I've had a number of clients who have questioned whole life insurance. One in particular decided to buy term insurance and invest the difference in mutual funds. That's worked well for him."

- "One of my older clients was wondering how to provide for her sister, much like you . . . she decided to set up a living trust."

In all cases, generic examples can be used to answer clients' questions, to provide additional information, to overcome resistance, and to motivate. Also, generic examples provide you an excellent opportunity to use your professional experiences as a source of financial possibilities for clients.

Using Your Voice. Using your voice refers to using voice inflection, intonation, volume, and speech rate to make suggestions or to emphasize important concepts. This natural part of the communication process is most effective when you *mark* your words. Marking is a process whereby you highlight certain words or phrases and thereby place emphasis on their meaning. This is done by exaggerating voice inflection, intonation, volume, or speech rate. People who have developed this use of marking can make suggestions indirectly and seed ideas in the listener. When you walked into the house as a youngster and a parent said your name in a loud clear voice, you automatically knew you were in trouble. Very often when parents want a child to listen carefully, they will raise or lower their voices.

This marking of words to emphasize points can be done in many ways. For example, consider this excerpt: "At this agency we try to help you *practice* good money management. Come in and let us show you *what you've* got to gain from what we have *learned* about making your money grow." The words in italics seem to make sense as they are written. Read the sentences out loud and place emphasis on the words that are italicized. Then read only the italicized words. You will notice that they form a sentence which suggests that you practice the skills and concepts you have learned while reading this book.

Consider this second example:

> "In these times of high inflation it's hard to maintain your ability to buy. We want to *look into* managing your finances to your best advantage. *Copies of* investment analyses are available from our *Financial Planning* staff. Why not let us *guide* you toward financial independence."

Again, notice that several words are italicized. When you read these words, you will notice an idea has been seeded to have you look into copies of a book entitled *Financial Planning Guide*.

The spoken word can be emphasized in the same way as the written word above. In talking to a client you might say, "I believe that it is important for you to consider a regular investment program, one in which you *invest* a minimum of *$100 per month*." In this statement, the words *invest $100 per month* are emphasized through voice inflection or volume. Emphasis on these words would seed the idea that the client should regularly invest $100 per month.

The process of using your voice can be used to seed ideas, as above, make suggestions, encourage client actions, motivate new behaviors, or to acknowledge past events. With practice, financial planners can control a very important communicative skill.

Using Stories. Using stories to teach or illustrate points is a natural process. The use of stories has been one of the most powerful teaching techniques of all the great leaders in history. Jesus taught primarily through the use of parables, short teaching stories. The same is true of Buddha and other great religious leaders. This normal process can be applied to the financial planning process as well. Using short stories to illustrate points can be used for a variety of purposes.

►*To establish relationships*. As we have discussed, building an effective relationship with clients is vital. The relationship should be characterized by openness, honesty, and trust. You can set the tone for relationships by sharing with your clients several short stories about the way you have worked with other clients. This accomplishes several important things. First, it communicates to your clients how you would like to work with them and shares your working style with them. Second, you can use your early story-telling times as a means of client assessment. If you carefully watch clients as you relate several stories about different clients in differing situations, you will be able to determine which clients are most apt to respond to specific approaches. Consider the following interchange as an example of this point:

Client: I'd like to set up a trust right away.

Financial professional: I know you understand a lot about trusts, but it's a little hard to jump into this cold, so let me give you some idea of trusts other clients have established. I had one client who wanted to protect his and his first wife's children. He went with a Q-tip Trust. Another client, anxious to minimize estate taxes, combined marital and nonmarital trusts. Still another client found the generation-skipping trust to be most appropriate.

In the above example the professional must tell the story *and* observe the client's reactions to each of the three segments. Usually, a client will give some indication of which of the client stories is most like him. The client will do this nonverbally. The client may frown or shake his head *no* to one example, while smiling, leaning forward, or nodding *yes* to another. These actions provide clues as to which approach is most appropriate for this client. If the client does not provide a nonverbal reaction or the professional advisor is unable to observe the differences in nonverbal behavior, all is not lost. The professional can follow the story with a simple question, "Which of these clients appears to be most like you?" In either case the story can be used to assess the kinds of trusts the client is interested in and the client's motivations.

▸*To seed ideas*. There may be times when you notice clients lack information or seem to have their minds made up in a certain way. You can use stories to seed ideas for them to consider. For example, you might say to a client, "In our discussion of limited partnerships, I was reminded of a friend of mine who wanted to put his money to work with little risk . . . He too considered certain limited partnerships . . . but then he realized he could get a steady return on his money through triple A rated bonds."

Obviously, in this example you could suggest investing in any vehicle you wish the client to consider. Through this process, you can make suggestions without raising the client's defenses. It is merely a story about some other client. If it has meaning to the present client, then she will accept the idea. If it doesn't have meaning for the client, she will ignore it as an interesting little anecdote.

▸*To suggest alternative ways of acting.* You might tell clients several stories about other clients and their success with particular financial strategies. This will indirectly suggest areas for them to consider. For instance, you might say, "One client I had was concerned about making adequate provisions for his family if he died. So he established a trust fund for each of his children and one for his wife." This *story* could be used to indirectly suggest that trust funds are good, as well as to suggest several kinds of trust funds the client might want to consider.

▸*To motivate clients.* A special use of stories is to motivate clients to act. There are two ways of doing this. First, you can tell clients stories about some of your clients or people you have known who have made bad decisions and who have had disastrous experiences because they didn't plan or didn't use their resources appropriately. By implication you suggest to clients that if they continue in the same vein they will have disastrous results as well. The danger in telling only disastrous stories is that clients may dismiss them as not applicable to them. The second way to use stories to motivate is to tell clients several stories about former clients who have had both successes and failures. By alternating or incorporating both positive and negative examples you can accomplish two things. You can, of course, motivate clients to act and you can suggest some possible investment ideas at the same time. Again, as mentioned above, the use of stories to motivate creates a "no lose" situation for you. If the stories have any meaning to the client, he will isolate the meaning that is right for him. If the story doesn't tap some part of his representational map, the stories become nothing more than interesting anecdotes. In either case no harm is done.

The principle involved in using stories is that clients are given an opportunity to meaningfully identify with characters in the story and apply their own meaning. You do not have to tell clients directly what it is they should or should not do. You can, however, use stories to offer suggestions, make recommendations, and seed ideas to be used in the future. Very often, after clients have heard stories like these, they will return with some new ideas about their situation, ideas which were, most often, suggested in the story. The ideas then belong to the clients, who are more likely to follow through on them.

CHAPTER 8

The Setting for Communication

In this chapter we will elaborate on a number of variables which affect the professional financial relationship. We will examine the physical conditions of the communicative interaction and the importance of your personal appearance. In addition, we will examine the related variables of time, sound, use of auxiliary personnel, and use of clients' records.

Physical Environment. The physical environment, although not the most crucial variable in an interaction, is important. An atmosphere that is comfortable, that allows for privacy, and that uses space in a nonthreatening manner can help you communicate more easily with clients. The following are some of the basic elements that are important in this regard.

Location. Where you meet a client can be quite influential in determining your personal comfort, your client's comfort, and what you can accomplish with the client. Generally speaking, three possibilities exist. You can meet your clients in your personal or professional setting, you can meet them in their home or place of work, or you can meet them in a neutral setting. All three possibilities have advantages and disadvantages, and all three are related to the power of space. Consider the following example:

> Jim, a high school student, sought out the school counselor's office. He wanted advice on how to resolve a conflict with his parents over his plans for after graduation. In this particular school, the counselor's office is entered by passing through the principal's waiting room. On his way to the counselor's office, Jim walked past students who had been sent to the principal for disciplinary reasons.

In this example, it is quite possible for Jim to be influenced negatively by the location of the counselor's office. He could easily think that the counselor represented the same kind of authority as that of a principal because of the proximity of the two offices. (Although this *might* be true, in most school counseling situations this would be an inappropriate assumption.) As a result of Jim's assumption, the counselor would have to overcome a defensiveness on Jim's part that would be detrimental to the success of their counseling relationship.

The point is that the location of one's office can be *influential*. If clients have to walk too many flights of stairs, search down long corridors for the right office, or meet in an open area near the secretarial area, this may have a negative effect which must be overcome each time the client comes to see you.

> ⋙**THE POWER OF PLACE**→ In the professional world, offices in the mainstream of traffic and corner offices confer the greatest influence. In the corporate world, offices that are higher and larger confer the greatest power. As a professional, you should be aware of the "influence" or "power" the location of your office carries and, if you have a choice, be careful in establishing where you locate yourself.

Remember that all locations have potentially positive or negative aspects. In our example, for instance, the counselor's office may be "bad" because it has the potential for establishing inappropriate student expectations. Yet, it may be quite "good" from other perspectives, for example, access to records, access to other professionals, or convenience for staff. It is important that both positive and negative aspects be considered and that you make choices that maximize the positives while diminishing the negatives.

To do this, you must consider two sets of needs that are affected by your choice: the psychological comfort of your client and your own professional needs. In general, clients will feel psychologically safe in a variety of settings and are able to adapt to different professional atmospheres. In some situations, however, clients will feel less comfortable in a "foreign" environment and will be more reserved in their communication. Be aware of this possibility and, whenever it is convenient, provide clients an opportunity to meet with you in a place where they are psychologically comfortable.

Letting clients choose the meeting place may pose some difficulty. For instance, you may find it more convenient to meet clients at your office because of less travel time, access to secretarial assistance, availability of client records, proximity to computers or duplicating equipment, or other reasons. Your needs for outside resources must be taken into account as well as clients' needs for psychological safety. Whenever possible, you can try to satisfy both conditions. On those rare occasions in which you cannot satisfy your needs and client needs, it is better for your relationship if you meet client needs for psychological comfort.

If you do choose to meet with clients in their environment, be aware that certain advantages and disadvantages will exist. When you meet clients in their home or workplace, the chances of them being psychologically comfortable are increased. It may be easier to establish a relationship, to develop professional trust, and to move toward satisfying client goals. All of these outcomes are quite positive. From another perspective, however, you may find this arrangement to be awkward. In addition to the negative consequences mentioned above regarding lack of access to resources, you may find that the client's environment can be less conducive to communication. It is possible that your clients will be interrupted with business concerns if you meet in their office or with family concerns if you meet in their homes. These negative aspects may or may not override positive aspects of meeting with your clients in their world. In any event, consider both positive and negative possibilities and make your decision with client needs in mind.

Finally, you could meet with your clients in a neutral setting such as a restaurant, a club, or a golf course. Like the previous meeting places, these neutral areas have the potential to be positive or negative. Usually, neutral areas can be chosen that are psychologically comfortable and helpful in establishing and maintaining a positive communicative relationship. In addition to providing this comfort, neutral areas can place you and your client on an equal footing. Both of you would be removed from the security of your personal surroundings. This can facilitate communication because it psychologically frees both of you to share in an equal manner by reducing influential status expectations.

Many of the negatives apparent in both of the previous possibilities are also apparent in neutral meeting areas. That is, you may still need resources that are not readily available, you may be interrupted frequently, or, in a general sense, the environment may not be totally conducive to effective communication.

Space. In Chapter 2 we presented a number of social implications of space and how interpersonal positioning influences what is communicated. We'd like to build on this understanding by relating it to how you arrange and decorate your office. The floor plan you use to organize office furniture, the colors and texture of furniture you choose, and your use of evidence that attests to your professional competence are all important in establishing an atmosphere that will facilitate communication. Although shape and positioning of office furniture are often overlooked as variables in communication, both are extremely important.

In examining furniture floor plans, three elements should be kept in mind—the shape of the furniture, seating arrangements, and general positioning of the furniture in the room. In general, round, square, and oval tables or desks can be used to create atmospheres of equality. By contrast, rectangular tables or desks are more likely to create status differentiation. In Figure 8.A, both individuals have positions of equal "power" in that neither person is sitting at the "head" of the table.

Figure 8.A

By contrast, in Figure 8.B, the individual sitting at the end of the table has more "power" than people sitting at the sides of the table. The "power" that occurs is a result of the end person's positioning, which allows him or her to establish and maintain eye contact with all other individuals at the table, a difficult task for the rest of the people at the table.

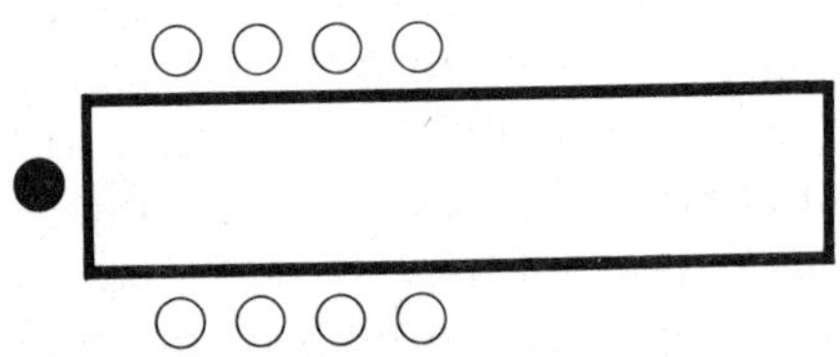

Figure 8.B

Now, apply this concept to selection of your desk and your arrangement of chairs. First, if you choose a round desk, you will establish an atmosphere that can lead to equality of participation and responsibility more easily than if you choose a rectangular desk. Let's assume, however, that you do choose a rectangular desk. Where should you place chairs around your desk? To answer this question you should determine what you hope to accomplish in your professional relationships and consider the following classifications of seating arrangements: If you have the responsibility for collecting on defaulted loans, Figure 8.C would provide you the greatest "power."

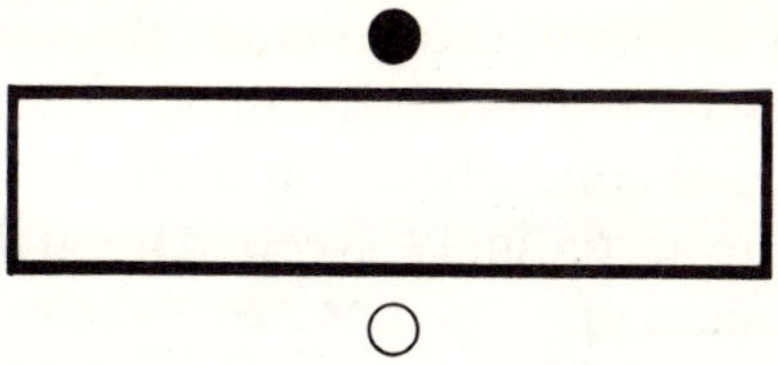

Figure 8.C

In the competitive arrangement, your seat commands the environment by using the desk as a source of "power" by providing a physical barrier between you and your client.

▸If your goal is planning rather than collection, the following arrangement (Figure 8.D) would be more appropriate.

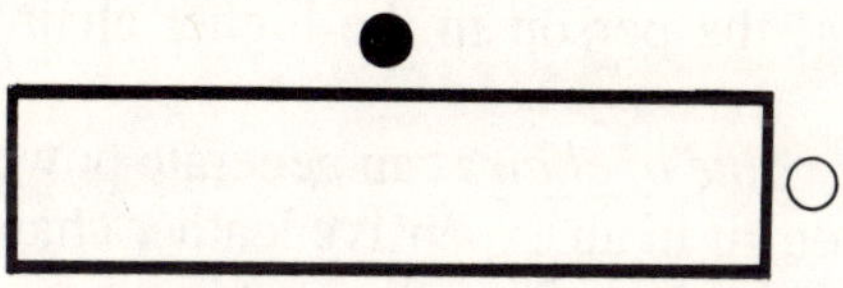

Figure 8.D

In the cooperative arrangement, the corner of the desk offers the client some security while establishing an atmosphere conducive to equality.

▸If your goal is neither collection nor planning, but rather counseling, you might consider Figure 8.E, in which both you and your client are removed from the influence of the desk.

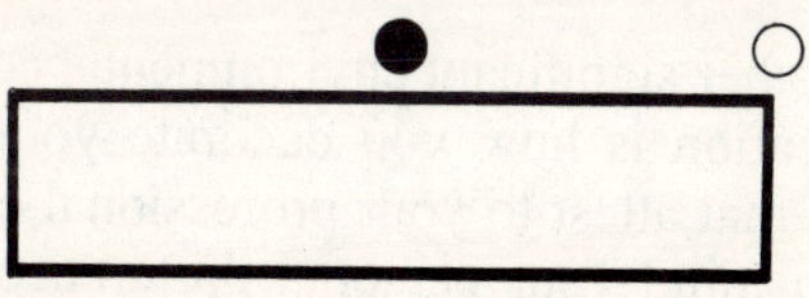

Figure 8.E

In the co-optive arrangement, both of you have equal "power" and equal responsibility.

▸An additional seating arrangement is possible (Figure 8.F). However, it is seldom used in professional interactions.

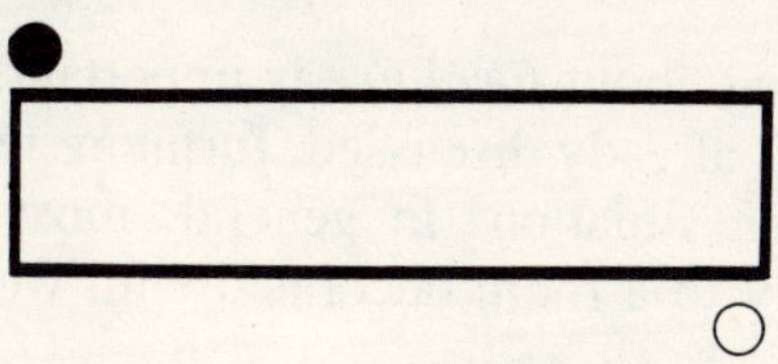

Figure 8.F

In most professional communications either the competitive or cooperative arrangements are preferred. Examine what you hope to accomplish and what type of atmosphere you wish to establish, and then arrange your furniture accordingly. Keep in mind that in doing so you can arrange for client options. For instance, you can place chairs in a variety of places and let your clients choose where they *want* to sit.

Power can also be generated in other ways through the physical environment.

▸ *Relative height* is one source. When one person is standing and another is sitting, the person standing will generally have more power. When applying this concept to seating, if one person's chair is higher than another's, the person in the higher chair will have greater influence.

▸ The *comparative value of chairs* can generate power or influence. For instance, if you sit in an expensive leather chair and your client sits in an inexpensive cloth chair, you can have greater influence.

▸ The *positioning of chairs* in the room can be a source of power. If your chair faces the door to the room, you will have greater influence than your client.

Obviously, to control the greatest power in communications, you would try to employ as many of these concepts as possible. Conversely, to establish an equal relationship you would utilize these concepts to minimize the potential influence of furniture arrangement.

Office Decor. Another significant environmental consideration in effective communication is how you decorate your office and how you display items that attest to your professional competence. In this regard, keep in mind your personal preferences, your clients' needs, and your professional goals. For example, a physical atmosphere that is *sterile* may interfere with your ability to develop a relationship with clients; whereas one that is too *homey* may give clients the idea that you are not professionally competent. The development of an atmosphere that will be most helpful will depend on your use of furniture, colors, decorations, textures, and professional acquisitions.

▸ Almost everything about *furniture* is important. In addition to furniture positioning, already discussed, furniture texture, style, and location impact the situation. In general, most people will respond more positively to a room decorated with wood furniture and natural fibers such as wool or cotton than to a room decorated with metal or plastic furniture and artificial fibers or synthetics. If your office is large enough, you could use this knowledge by adding a sofa or easy chair to soften the atmosphere and provide alternative arrangements for your professional discussions. The following arrangement of furniture (Figure 8.G) could be used to provide a psychologically pleasing, flexible environment.

Figure 8.G

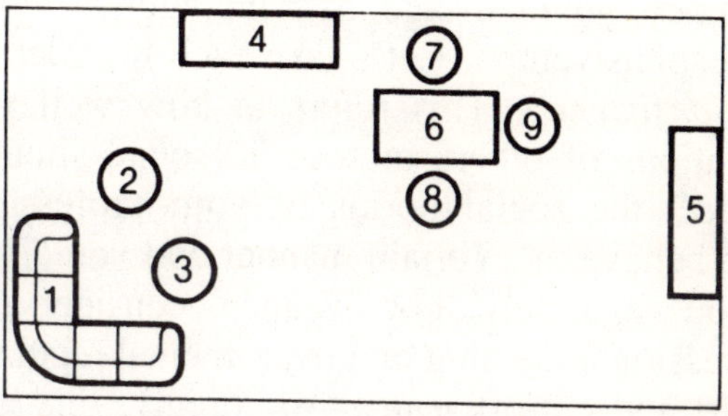

KEY
1-SOFA
2-EASY CHAIR
3-TABLE
4-5-BOOKCASES
6-DESK
7-DESK CHAIR
8-9-OFFICE CHAIRS

▸In addition to furniture arrangement and texture, *color* is influential. Most people feel psychologically comfortable in rooms that use pastel or earth-tone colors. Vibrant colors may be more energizing, but are less acceptable for professional relationships. In this regard, wall hangings of a subtle nature are viewed positively by a higher percentage of people than bold, highly creative designs.

▸*Natural elements* such as plants, flowers, and small trees add significantly to the psychological comfort of an office.

▸It is important to include *evidence of your professional accomplishment and competency* in your decorating plan. Items such as licenses, diplomas, certificates of achievement, and professional awards should be openly displayed. You could even have copies of published articles on a table in the waiting area. It is important for clients to see evidence that you are skilled at your profession. Professional credentials, openly displayed, set the stage for open professional communication.

Personal Variables. The way you are viewed by clients depends on your reputation, your personal communicative style, your level of expertise, and your personal appearance. All of these variables are under your control. The first three result from your professional preparation and personal style of delivery. Your appearance is somewhat different. This variable is based on your social consistency, your carriage, hygiene, clothes, communicative ability, and responsiveness. Let's take each in order:

Social Consistency. This refers to how well you meet the social expectations of others in specific social situations or how well you reflect the social norms of your profession. If others expect you to behave in a certain manner and you don't, they may respond to you negatively. For instance, consider a banker who attends a professional meeting on governmental regulations dressed in a sweatshirt and cut-off jeans. Admittedly, this may be a far-fetched example, but the point is that certain behavior is professionally unacceptable, some in a dramatic way, some in a more subtle manner. In this example, the banker is dressed inappropriately for the professional situation. However, if a picnic were held to allow bankers and government personnel to meet informally, then the banker in our example *would be* dressed appropriately. By contrast, attending the picnic in a three-piece, navy blue pinstriped suit might be quite inappropriate!

> ⋙**SOCIAL EXPECTATIONS**→ We have expectations that are based on our experiences and familiarity with specific social groups and specific situations. We learn to know when a behavior is appropriate and when it isn't. These social expectations are the basis for what is acceptable in the above example and in all of the following personal variables.

Personal variables such as carriage, clothes, and hygiene all affect how others see you. People can use these three variables to form an opinion about you even without communicating with you.

Carriage. Some individuals walk with their heads held high, their shoulders back, and an alert look on their face, while others walk in a slouched manner and look at the ground as they walk. As you observe people, you might classify some as proud, others as shy, pompous, or relaxed. You form your opinions from these subtle clues that people emit. You then classify people into categories. Your opinions of and possibly your actions toward people are based upon your classifications.

Clothes. A second observation that you probably will make revolves around how people are dressed. Appropriateness of professional dress follows subtle, informal rules. Through your professional training and experience, you have probably learned most of these rules. There may be situations, however, in which you don't know what is appropriate and, consequently, you may feel out of place, ill at ease, or embarrassed. When in doubt, a conservative clothing choice will prove to be the safer course. Steering clear of bright colors, bold patterns, and unconventional styles ensures a more professional image. (Professional women, in particular, will find this rule of thumb useful in narrowing their generally wide range of clothing choices.)

In addition to the choice of appropriate clothes, how you wear clothes is important. Clothes that are too large, too tight, or unpressed create a negative image, as do shoes that need polish or a shirt that is not tucked in. Clothes need to be appropriate for the situation, be properly tailored and cleaned, and be worn in an acceptable fashion.

Hygiene. Closely tied to how one wears clothing is personal hygiene. A professional who neglects this important area communicates a negative or unsavory image to clients. The areas to be attended to most diligently are the hair, fingernails, teeth, breath, and body odor. How you wear and maintain your hair is an obvious reflection of your personal self-image and professional awareness. It is true that the subtle rules for professional hair style differ slightly. Whereas bankers, lawyers, doctors, and business executives have one acceptable style, college professors have another, and artists still another.

Despite moderate differences in informal rules set by your profession, almost all professions expect cleanliness. To be slightly outside the informal rules for your profession can be tolerated. To have unclean hair usually is not tolerated and probably will result in a negative image. Dirty fingernails, unsightly teeth, bad breath, and body odor can lead others to have a negative image of the offender. The message frequently transferred through all of these personal variables is "if they don't care enough about themselves to comb their hair, clean their fingernails, take care of their teeth, cleanse their breath, or to wash away body odor, how could they possibly care enough about me to attend to my needs in a competent manner?'' Personal sloppiness communicates an uncaring attitude that clients generalize to professional encounters.

Communicative ability. Communicative ability has a number of dimensions. First, *when* you choose to talk is important. Do you, for instance, talk when you should be listening? Do you interrupt other people as they talk? Do you finish others' sentences for them? Are you impatient while others present their ideas? If you are normal, and we assume that you are, you probably answered ''yes'' to some of these questions. You might ask yourself, ''Well, what do good communicators do?'' One answer to this question could be that good communicators attempt to listen attentively to their clients and to talk when their clients have finished what they have to say.

In addition to when you talk, *what* you have to say is important. The statement, ''I thought he was a fool, and when he opened his mouth it removed all doubt,'' attests to the negative consequence of inappropriate talk. Your verbal communication should be purposeful and appropriate to the professional situation.

Third, *how* you talk is important. How rapidly you speak, how loudly you talk, how much emphasis you put on words, how well you enunciate, your diction, and whether you have an accent all influence how much your clients get from what you say. In general, moderation in most of these aspects is best. That is, most people prefer to listen to someone who speaks without ''too much'' speed, loudness, pitch or tonality variance, or accent. In most professional situations, a low-keyed, straightforward manner of presentation is the most productive.

Interpersonal responsiveness. Your personal method of responding to clients is important. How you use eye contact, how and when you smile, how and when you nod your head all can communicate attentiveness and interest. It is important for you to know how and when to respond so that you can respond in a manner that is consistent with your personal desires and professional goals.

Finally, your interaction with clients probably begins and ends with a subtle form of communication that can create a positive or negative attitude. This form of communication is the handshake. The manner in which you shake hands can have an influence on what a client thinks about you, and conversely, what you think about your clients. In discussing your communicative ability, we suggested that most clients prefer a moderate approach. We make the same observation with regard to handshakes. It is important to be firm but not overly assertive. A feeble grip will suggest weakness on your part, whereas too powerful a grip can lead your clients to question your intent. We suggest that you adopt a moderate grip that will communicate concern without being overbearing.

Final Considerations. It is obvious that many things can and do influence professional communications. In previous sections of this chapter we addressed those that where related to physical and personal variables. In this section we discuss a number of elements that are closely related to both, but more specifically to the environment in which communication takes place. In this regard, the use of time, sounds, auxiliary personnel, and clients' records are addressed.

▸*Time* is a finite element and consequently extremely important in communications. Probably most of your clients are busy people. If you do not respect this possibility and do not use your client's time in an efficient manner, you will rob them of an important commodity. Time can be used inappropriately by keeping clients waiting; by failing to answer their telephone calls in a timely manner; by being inflexible in your schedule; by failing to provide an able backup when you cannot attend to clients' needs; or, more simply, by answering the phone call of one client while serving another. When professionals use time inappropriately, they communicate a lack of respect for their clients. In essence, they communicate, "My time is important; yours is not!" Obviously, we suggest that you guard against this possibility and use time to convey respect for your clients by attending to their needs in an efficient, timely manner.

▸*Sound*, like time, can be used in a productive or negative way. Low-volume classical or semi-classical background music facilitates communication. Consequently, this type of music provides an excellent backdrop for professional conversations. From a negative perspective, loud music, unusually noisy voices, or disquieting background sounds can interfere with communications and should be avoided.

▸A third element to consider is the communicative benefits of appropriately trained *auxiliary personnel*. In most professional situations clients seek information when they feel a need for it. In your case you may be able to provide your clients a consistently timely response. If you cannot, however, auxiliary personnel such as a knowledgeable secretary or assistant can be used to provide clients pertinent information when they need it. They can extend your professional usefulness by allowing you to communicate with more than one client at a time—the one you communicate with directly and the one you communicate with indirectly through your auxiliary personnel. Trained auxiliary personnel can help you to communicate that your professional service is convenient, efficient, and able to respond to clients' needs.

▸ Finally, properly maintained, readily accessible *records* foster communications. Clients expect you to be knowledgeable about your professional field and able to use information in their behalf. Further, clients probably expect you to understand their personal situation, to be able to apply information from your professional field in general, and to be able to make personal recommendations that are based on your knowledge of the field and the client. This can occur only if you maintain accurate records and have a system for obtaining information in an efficient manner. When clients see that your records are professionally developed, accurately updated, confidentially maintained, and readily accessible to you, they "get the message" that you are an efficient, competent professional. This, we assume, is exactly what you would like to communicate!

CHAPTER 9

The Multiple Interview

We have discussed communication and interviewing principles and skills as they apply to two-person interviews. Many times, however, you will interview or communicate with more than one person at a time. Probably the most common occurrence will be when you work with couples. In this chapter we will discuss the special concerns you must keep in mind when dealing with more than one person. How do you pace, motivate, explore, and deal with the conflict of two or more distinct client personalities?

Multiple Communication Patterns. When two people interact a pattern of communication exists which relates to the flow of information between the two. As discussed previously, the output from one person becomes the input for the second and *vice versa*. There is mutual influence in that one person's outputs place expectations on the form and kind of output of the second person.

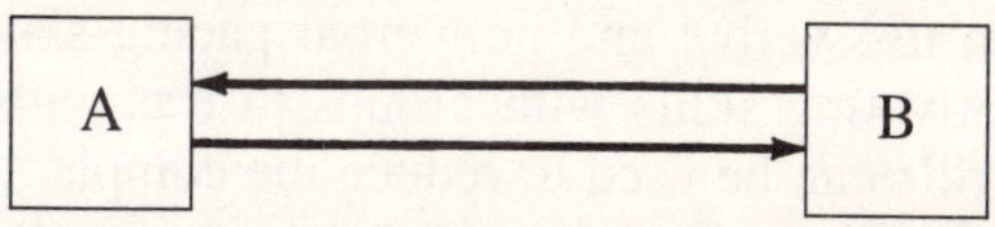

In *multiple* communicative interactions the patterns of communication and the potential for influence expand rapidly. When a third person is added to an existing two-person interaction, a three-way pattern of communication results. If we assume that the financial professional is at the tip of the following triangle, in position C, there is an interaction between both clients and the financial professional. In addition, there is potential for a fourth pattern, where any of the three persons, in one message, directs communication to both of the other two persons.

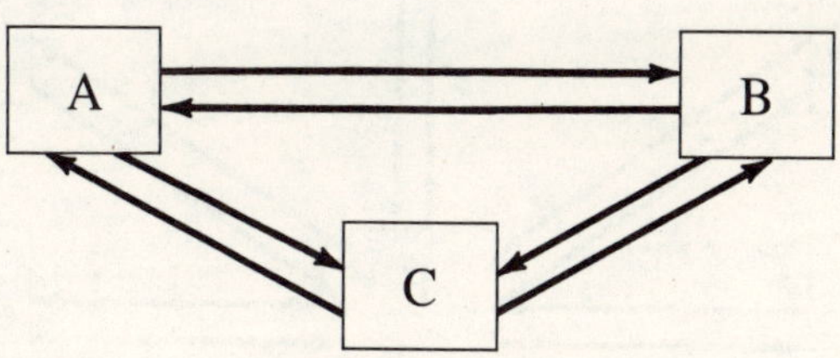

Adding of more people to the interaction increases the number of communicative patterns. For example, when a fourth person is added to the group there is the potential for at least seven distinct patterns to develop, i.e., six different pair configurations and one that represents an address to the entire group from any of the four group members, plus groups of three interactors.

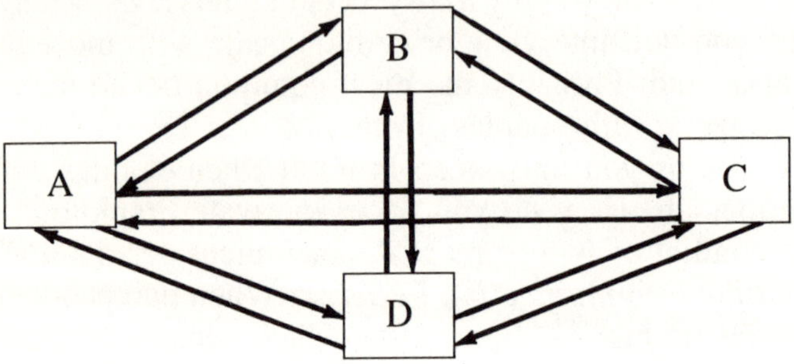

While potential patterns of communication and influence increase with each additional person, interviewing and communication skills necessary to deal with such complexities remain constant. You can use verbal and nonverbal pacing skills, exploring skills, and motivating skills with groups just as with individuals. These same skills can be used to reduce the complexity of interaction and to control patterns of communication. Each of the above diagrams shows the number of *potential* patterns. However, an effective communicator can control the number of *active* patterns by controlling the centrality of communication. That is, an effective communicator can establish himself or herself as the center of communication flow. Geometrically, this would look a little like a wheel, with all communication being directed through the hub.

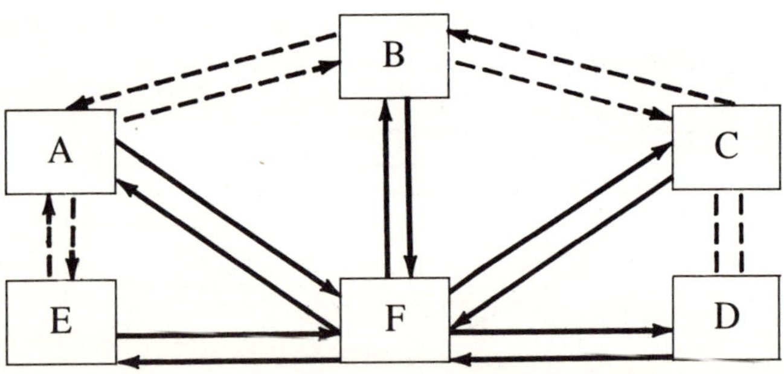

Notice in this figure that the person in the middle has the potential to act as gatekeeper. Most communication, indicated by the solid lines, is directed by and funneled through the person in the center. There is little communication, indicated by the broken lines, among the other participants. The difference between the figures formed by the two sets of lines is roughly equivalent to the difference between a group discussion and a teaching situation. In a group discussion each participant can take an active part and talk or respond to every other person. In teacher–student situations, teachers usually control communication so that it is channeled through them.

We recommend that in professional financial encounters you establish patterns of communication similar to the teaching model. We are not implying that you should become a "teacher," but that it is easier to control communicative patterns if you become the hub of the process. This allows you to control the focus of communication while allowing group members to openly communicate with each other. In this approach, you have more control over both the content and the process of communication.

Skills are applied in a slightly different manner in multiple communicative interactions. In the standard two-person interview, skills are used to focus on information and the manner in which the client processes information. Although you must still focus on information in the multiple interview, you will probably need to deal more with the manner in which your clients communicate about the information under discussion. This shift in focus occurs for a number of reasons.

First, in the multiple interview you must focus on the needs of more than one person. This automatically limits your ability to attend to any *one* person. You may miss information being transmitted through subtle clues of voice inflection, body gestures, or space usage. The data you have about any one person will be much less than what you would gather in an individual interview, while the information you have about the group will increase.

Second, the group or multiple format prevents you from responding to every client need. You must "spread" yourself around by responding to the needs of all members of the group. To do this, the level or intensity of your response to any one person will be less than it would be in an individual interaction.

In essence, the multiple interview forces you to be aware of the group at the expense of any one individual.

Pacing. Verbal pacing skills of restating, paraphrasing, and summarizing are used in the multiple communicative interaction much as in individual interactions. You can restate, paraphrase, or summarize any individual statement made by any client. You can also summarize, from time to time, the discussion that has taken place among all participants. By contrast, the use of nonverbal pacing in multiple interactions demands further discussion.

When you nonverbally pace, you attempt to match another person's important nonverbal behavior to communicate acceptance, warmth, and understanding. This helps build trust, which is necessary for effective relationships. But whom do you nonverbally pace when talking to more than one person at a time?

Realistically you can't nonverbally pace everyone. Yet, the process of nonverbal pacing in multiple interactions is rather simple. You nonverbally pace the person who is talking. You will find that when you nonverbally pace the speaker he or she will tend to direct more communication toward you than to others in the multiple situation.

As you pace each speaker you *will* become the hub of the communicative pattern. And this will allow you to use your own nonverbal behavior to lead and direct the flow of communication. For example, one of the authors was counseling a couple who were having minor difficulties in their relationship. The meeting took place in late afternoon during the summer. The wife was a teacher who was then on vacation. She came to the interview dressed in casual slacks and a blouse. The husband came to the interview, directly from work, dressed in a three-piece suit. The wife sat in a relaxed manner in her chair. She eventually slid down, stretched her feet out in front of her, and rested her head on the back of the chair. Her husband, by contrast, sat erect, with both feet on the floor, and clasped the arms of the chair.

As frequently happens in counseling couples, each spouse began by sharing with the author his or her perception of the relationship. Both the husband and wife directed most of their dialogue to the author, who was sitting in front and between them. The author selectively nonverbally paced each speaker. When the wife spoke, the author leaned back in his chair and matched her general body orientation. When the husband spoke, the author sat erect in his chair and focused his attention on him. The author said little during this initial part of the interview, responding most frequently by using the verbal pacing skills of paraphrasing and summarization.

At one point in the interview, the author felt that it was important for the couple to talk directly to each other rather than through him. The author accomplished this by leaning forward in his chair and alternately looking at the wife and the husband. The author repeated the process by looking at the husband and then at the wife, paused, and looked between them. After a few seconds had elapsed, the wife sat up straighter in her chair, leaned forward toward her husband, and began to address him directly. The husband, without hesitation, responded directly to her.

In this example, the author used verbal and nonverbal pacing to establish an effective relationship. Through verbally and nonverbally pacing each speaker the author became the hub of the communication. After trust was established, the author was able to lead the couple to communicating with each other. The author did this by changing his nonverbal behavior and by nonverbally directing the couple, through his focus on a point between the couple, to come together.

Exploring. Exploring techniques can be used in the multiple interview in the same manner that they are used in individual interactions. However, in multiple communicative interactions, exploration skills also can be used to focus on the clients' communication process. This requires you to pay attention to *how* group members respond to what is being said as well as to the information that is being shared.

For example, in working with a couple, you might notice that when one person is talking, the other person nonverbally expresses emotion to what is being said. Whether the person signals confusion, anger, frustration, happiness, disagreement, agreement, or another emotion, you can facilitate communication by being alert to these responses, by examining the interaction to determine what specifically is triggering these responses, by observing the interaction process in its entirety, and by leading group members to focus on issues that foster particular responses. For example, consider the following:

Financial professional: I noticed that while your spouse was talking you didn't seem to agree. Tell me what you disagree with.

In this example, the financial professional has first shared an observation and then used an imperative lead to explore how the person feels about what is being said. In the example that follows, the financial professional notices that one of the clients looks confused as the other talks.

Financial professional: I think I understand what you are trying to say. It would help me and maybe your spouse if you would tell us a little more about what you mean by a secure investment.

In this example, the financial professional has asked for concept clarification and has brought the spouse into the exploration. This broader form of exploration occurs because the financial professional notices that the spouse has nonverbally expressed confusion.

In general, there are four major sources of conflict in multiple interactions. They include the following, and will be discussed here:

- Differences in male-female communication styles
- Differences in learning styles
- Differences in basic needs
- Differences in values

As discussed previously, males and females frequently express their thoughts in different ways. For example, *in general*, females are more likely to respond to the specifics of a statement, while males are more likely to respond to the overall message being conveyed. In a multiple interaction that has both male and female participants, *differences in communication styles* can lead to misunderstanding. You, as a facilitative financial professional, can help individuals to communicate more effectively by helping them to recognize and bridge their individual differences. Consider the following interchange as an example of this point.

Financial professional: If we choose the direction that we've been discussing, you may feel that your resources are being stretched too thin. In my opinion, this would last for a short time and then you would start to feel that you could handle it okay.

Martha might ask, "How long would we feel this heavy burden?" whereas Dan might say, "In the long run it looks like we could benefit from this."

To be most helpful, the financial professional should respond to both, possibly in the following manner.

Financial professional: We do have two situations, the short term and the long term. . . . Martha, in response to your question, I believe that you'd feel the financial burden for less than six months. . . . Dan, I would agree with you; I think that if you are willing to put up with the financial difficulty for the six months you will reap substantial long-term gains.

In this interchange, the financial professional indicates an understanding of how both Martha and Dan view the problem, acknowledges both clients, and attends to differences in their individual communicative styles.

Differences in clients' learning styles is a second potential source for communicative difficulty. Consider the following:

Financial professional: Tell me what type of investment you would consider at this point.

Mary: I would like an investment that makes sense given all of our assets and the goals that we've established.

John: Umm hmm....but I feel that it is very important that whatever we do we don't get bound up or tied in knots!

In this interchange Mary's learning style seems to be auditory, whereas John's appears to be kinesthetic. Mary's statements reflect *thinking* about what needs to be done, while John's words are *action-oriented*. The financial professional, in working with these clients, should determine if these early statements represent how Mary and John communicate *generally*.

Once this is known, the financial professional can communicate more effectively with both persons by using their preferred style of communicating and can help Mary and John communicate more effectively with each other.

A third area of potential conflict results from *differences in individual needs*. Abraham Maslow suggests that individuals operate on a need hierarchy that incorporates five basic needs: a basic need for food, drink, and sexual contact; a need for security from the environment; a need for social contact and acceptance; a need for self-esteem; and a need for self-actualization. Not all individuals have the same need, or combination of needs, at the same time. Consequently, conflict can occur when two or more clients have different needs. For example, consider the following:

Financial professional: What type of investment is most appealing to you?

Wife: I'd like to put our money into something that has a good chance for growth. I'm interested in having our money make money so that we can do the things we've always wanted to do.

Husband: I think that we have to invest for our retirement. I want to make sure that when I retire we have enough to live on!

It is obvious in this interchange that the spouses have different needs. One is concerned with social or possibly self-esteem needs, while the other is concerned with security. The financial professional must be aware of these differences and help both clients to understand their needs and, possibly, to resolve their differences.

Finally, *differences in basic values* can lead to conflict in interpersonal interactions. The five basic values that we believe are important in financial communications revolve around issues of *power*, *status*, *love*, *security*, and *autonomy*. Consider the following statements that reflect financial values:

> Money should be used to control others! (power)
> Wealth allows me to belong to the "right" country club. (status)
> I want to use my financial resources to help the needy. (love)
> The greatest value of money is that I don't have to worry about the future. (security)
> Money allows me to do the things I want! (autonomy)

All of these values are displayed by individuals at one time or another. Yet, people behave in a manner that suggests that at least one is more important to them most of the time. Be on the alert for dramatic differences in your clients' value orientations and be ready to use communication skills to help resolve apparent differences.

In all of the potential conflict-producing circumstances described above, your role as a financial professional is constant. You must be alert to client differences and be able to facilitate communication between or among clients, effectively pace individuals verbally and nonverbally within the multiple interaction, and control the flow and direction of communication.

Dealing with Conflict. In addition to the sources of conflict mentioned above, four potentially hazardous situations can arise in multiple interviews. The first we call *Participant Observer*. In this situation, conflict erupts between or among clients, while the financial professional is left to observe the ensuing argument. The second we call *The Vise*, and it results in the financial professional being pressured from two sides at once. Usually it begins as a disagreement between two clients and frequently progresses to a second stage, a joint client attack on the well-intentioned financial professional. The third type of conflictual situation is *Getting Caught in the Middle*, where disagreements arise and the financial professional is asked to take sides. Finally, the fourth type is the *Multiple Attack*, which may occur when the interview includes three or more clients at the same time. We discuss each of these below and suggest ways they can be dealt with.

Participant Observer. This situation is the most common of the four. As clients discuss their situations their differing values, needs, learning styles, communicative styles, and goals can lead to verbally expressed conflict. While being a participant observer in the clients' conflict situation may be uncomfortable, it allows you to observe the process and to intervene to focus the discussion on problem resolution. The resolution will occur when you move clients to some common ground for examining the decision or problem under discussion. Below is an example of a financial professional who is left to observe a client couple's interaction.

Financial professional: Well, we have discussed a number of options, and I'm wondering what you two would like to do.

Bob: Yes. Well, I think we ought to really look into some of those technology investments you talked about. They sound like we would have a real potential for fast growth! I mean we could double our money real quick that way.

Pat: But Bob, those are so risky! I think it would be like giving our money away. I don't want to invest in something where we might lose all our money overnight!

Bob: Well, it's extra cash we have for investing. It's not like we will be in the poorhouse if we lose it. I want to invest in something where we have a chance of making it big.

Pat: We worked hard for that money, and I don't want to just throw it away! I think we should be a lot more conservative, investing in something where we will have a guarantee.

Bob: You sound as though the only thing you want to do with the money is put it in the bank.

Pat: You seem to want to make all the decisions!

. . . And so on.

Notice that in this interchange the financial professional has been on the sidelines as an observer. Besides the obvious feelings of embarrassment you might have watching the clients argue in front of you, there is the natural desire to want to help. If you do try to help, there is the danger of *Getting Caught in the Middle* or of being caught in *The Vise* and having both people vent their emotions on you. The key is to try to discover the clients' basic differences and help them to focus on resolving them.

In this interchange there are some obvious value and attitudinal differences between the two on how to invest their money. What is unclear is what the couple's goals are. It might be assumed that their differences in values and attitudes stem from differences in goals. The financial professional can test this possibility by focusing the discussion on goals.

Financial professional: It sounds as though both of you have strong feelings about how to invest your money. I'm wondering if you have discussed what you want to accomplish by investing. It would help me if we could spend a few minutes talking about your goals. Pat, what do you want to accomplish by investing?

Pat: What is most important to me is getting ready for the kids' college education and then having a nice nest egg so that we don't have to worry about money when we retire.

Financial professional: How about you, Bob?

Bob: Well, I figure that with both of us working we will be able to handle the college expenses out of our normal income, and we both have pretty good retirement plans at work. So I think we ought to invest our money so that we can buy and do things over and above our normal income and retirement.

Financial professional: That helps. On the surface it sounds like you want to go in different directions, and that may be where the disagreement is coming from. I'm wondering if they are really that different, though.

Pat: What do you mean?

Financial professional: Well, one way of approaching things is to invest your money to provide for both college and the nest egg you talked about. This would release more of your current income to buy the things Bob talked about. On the other hand, if you use ordinary income to cover the college expenses, you could use your investments to build a nest egg and to buy the things Bob wants. I'm wondering if you might do both.

The key to helping in this form of conflict is to identify underlying themes that the clients don't seem to be dealing with directly. In the example, the financial professional's hypothesis appeared to be accurate—the couple *does* have a difference of underlying goals.

The Vise. This form of conflict ultimately leads to an attack of the financial professional by both clients. Despite your best efforts, you may find yourself caught in *The Vise*. Let's return to the example above and see how that might happen.

Financial professional: It sounds as though both of you have strong feelings about how to invest your money. I'm wondering if you have discussed what you want to accomplish through investments. It would help me if we could spend a few minutes talking about your goals. Pat, what do you want to accomplish by investing?

Pat: Of course we've discussed our goals. We want to invest so that we can make our assets grow. Isn't that right, Bob?

Bob: Yeah! We know what we want to accomplish and we have the same goals. We want to get ahead of inflation!

As you can see, even your best efforts may turn a situation into a pattern in which the couple uses you to vent their emotions. The emotions usually are subconsciously intended for each other but the financial professional becomes an easy and safe target, safe in the sense that the couple won't have to deal with their emotions with each other. When you are caught in a vise the immediate goal is to move yourself back to the participant observer position so that any continued attacks will be between clients rather than directed toward you. Continuing with the dialogue:

Financial professional: There seems to be a lot of emotion tied up in this issue of how to invest your money. Bob, tell me, how do you think you should invest your money?

Bob (still attacking): Well I don't think it is a matter of goals. I want to invest in something where we have a chance of making it big. I don't mind taking a few chances.

Pat: Wait a minute, Bob! I don't want to take any big chances with our money. We need to save that for the kids' college education and . . .

Bob: I'm worried about the kids' education just as much as you are, but I want to make some money so that we can do things we can't do now.

Notice in this short interchange the financial professional did not respond directly to attacks that put her in a vise. Rather, she directed attention on the strong emotions being expressed and then focused back on what the couple wants to accomplish. As Bob expressed his desires, Pat then responded to what she didn't like in what Bob said. The attack was redirected to *the clients*, and then the financial professional moved again to the participant observer position.

At this point, the immediate goal should be to reduce conflict so that effective problem-solving can take place. The financial professional's first attempt was not successful. Remember the general principle, that if what you are doing isn't producing what you want, try something different. You can be fairly certain that if the financial professional repeats the original response, she will probably get a repeat of the initial reaction, an attack on her! As an example of trying something different, the financial professional might say the following:

Financial professional (looking for resolution): I guess there is a lot more emotion in this issue of how to invest than I thought. Let's see if we can find some common ground we can agree on and then go from there. One thing I heard both of you say is that you are concerned with the kids' college educations.

Pat: Well, yes. That is the most important thing to me right now.

Bob: Yeah, we need to know that we can provide them with whatever help we can. My folks helped me a lot through college, and I know it meant a lot to me.

Pat: My parents provided all the money for me to go to college and I think it was one of the best things they ever did for me.

Financial professional: This seems to be something you both feel very strongly about. But the difference seems to be how you want to accomplish it. . . .

The financial professional initially used a good summarizing response focused on how the couple was feeling. Then the communication was focused on reaching a common understanding where the discussion could begin anew. Again, in a multiple client situation, the skills used are the same as those used in one-to-one encounters, but the focus is often on the communicative process rather than on the content itself. When there is strong emotion being expressed in the communicative pattern, it is often most helpful to focus on the theme and the process rather than on defending yourself.

Getting Caught in the Middle. This form of conflict occurs when you are asked to take sides on an issue. Intuitively, you know that if you take sides, you are being used to convince one client how to think or act. You also know from experience that if you take sides you may alienate one of the clients. This situation usually begins with the clients each trying to pull you into his or her way of thinking. You would probably get the feeling that you were being pulled in two different directions at once. For example:

Bob: I think that we should invest in something that gives us the quickest potential for doubling our money. That way we can be sure of having money for the kids' education.

Pat: But if we put the money in a CD for three or more years we can get at least 6% and and it will be insured, and we wouldn't have to worry about losing it.

In this interchange, the spouses express their opinions, each in a different direction. At this point there probably will not be a direct overture for agreement from the financial professional. However, if the financial professional watches the nonverbal behavior closely, usually there will be some indirect bid for agreement: looking at the financial professional while making a point, nodding as a form of asking for a yes from the financial professional, or gesturing toward the financial professional when speaking. It is important that you do not respond verbally or nonverbally to these indirect bids. Any kind of response such as a nod that is intended to mean "I understand you," can be taken as agreement. If you do not respond nonverbally to the bids for agreement, you might hear something like the following:

Bob: Well (financial professional's name) knows that I'm right, because by putting our money in a guaranteed CD we will just keep up with inflation.

At this point the financial professional has a direct bid for agreement. She is being *caught in the middle*, by being asked to take sides. Her first move should be to move toward the participant observer position.

Financial professional: You both seem to have strong opinions on how to accomplish saving money for your kids' education. It sounds to me as though Pat needs a greater sense of security about investing and Bob would like to take more risks.

Bob: Well, if we don't take risks we won't ever get ahead of the game.

Pat: But if we take risks that are too big we might lose everything we have worked so hard for and jeopardize the money for college.

Financial professional: I'm wondering what you think about investments that have some risk but not the high risk that the technology stocks have.

In the first response the financial professional focused again on the process and feelings being expressed. Notice that the response slowed the conflict and moved the financial professional back to the participant observer position. In that position the financial professional could then focus on the underlying theme of "risk taking" as a basis for moving to resolve client conflict.

A second form of *Getting Caught in the Middle* can occur when two people give a third person contradictory advice. This can happen when a client consults with two different financial professionals. One professional may suggest one course of action, while the other suggests something entirely different. At this point the client might not know which way to turn.

You may experience this form of *Getting Caught in the Middle* when a client comes to you for a third opinion. Frequently clients will attempt to use you to decide for them. You may offer advice that agrees with one of the two previously consulted financial professionals or advice that is completely different. In either case, we recommend that you move yourself to the participant observer role and help clients to resolve their own conflict. For example:

Client: I have talked with several financial planners and I keep getting different stories. One told me that purchasing universal life insurance is the way to go, while another told me that it is better to purchase term insurance. Which do you think is better?

Financial professional: It can be very confusing trying to figure out which way to invest, and those two options are certainly viable. Have you figured out the relative costs and benefits of each?

The financial professional effectively sidesteps getting caught in the middle by focusing on the client's feelings and then redirects the communication to the client's responsibility to logically examine the situation. In this example, the client is being asked to evaluate the options as a basis for future decision making. The financial professional moved to the participant observer role and attempted to facilitate the client's problem solving. The financial professional avoided making the decision for the client or adding a third alternative; both actions could make the situation more confusing for the client. Again, the best approach usually is to move to the participant observer position from which you can facilitate client decision making and problem solving.

The Multiple Attack. This conflict situation occurs when you are attacked by three or more people at the same time. This situation can occur when you are making a group presentation to a group of clients, presenting ideas in a seminar setting, or even in making a presentation to a group of colleagues. As with the other forms of conflict, your first response should be directed at moving to the participant observer position. In this position, if the conflict continues, it will occur among participants rather than be directed at you. From this participant observer position, you can redirect attacks to underlying themes and move the discussion toward a common ground of understanding as a basis for resolution.

As an example of this process consider the following situation, in which a government official has been asked to discuss zoning regulations with a group of community realtors.

Official: The zoning regulations established in 1984 may have to be changed to accommodate the rapid growth in the western part of town.

John (realtor 1): I sure hope you plan to get that changed to allow multiple residential units out there. I can't see any reason to do otherwise!

Betty (realtor 2): Rezoning it for multiple residential units would be the worst thing you could do! You people have to get on the ball on this and rezone it for private homes.

Susan (realtor 3): We don't need any more areas of residence out there. What we need is to preserve our park system. You'd better keep that in mind!

It should be obvious in this situation that our harried government official is being attacked by three people, all with personal needs. If the official agrees with any of the three, he will immediately be attacked by the other two. To avoid this and to place himself in a position where he can be most helpful to the *entire* group, he should move to the participant observer position and redirect participant energies to underlying emotions and issues.

Official: I can see that you all have definite opinions about what might serve the city best. That's good, but it would be helpful to me to understand your points of view better. John, you seem to believe that multiple residential zoning is the way to go. Why don't you share with Betty and Susan why you think that is so important.

The official has set the stage for getting the three participants to talk directly to one another and has provided himself an opportunity to step back into a *participant observer* role. From here he can respond to "group" needs and direct the flow of communication.

This chapter shares the belief that you, as a financial professional, must be aware of potential sources of conflict, that you must be able to help clients to see ways of resolving conflicts, and that you must be prepared to focus on the process of communication. It is our belief that you will be most helpful to all members in a multiple interaction if you adopt the role of *participant observer* and control the process of communication.

CHAPTER 10

Decision Making and Problem Solving Strategies

In previous chapters we discussed communication techniques used to develop and maintain effective working relationships, techniques which provide the foundation for pacing, exploring, and motivating clients. In addition to the underlying principle of influence in the financial professional relationship, there is the immediate objective of helping clients achieve their goals. To accomplish this the financial professional must be involved in helping clients to solve problems and to make wise decisions. Specific techniques can be used to facilitate decision making and problem solving, and these utilize communication skills presented in previous chapters.

All decision making and problem solving strategies have strengths and weaknesses. Their relative merit depends on financial professionals' and clients' value judgments and learning styles. Thus, people who place a high value on rational thinking or who have an auditory learning style usually select systematic, logical strategies. People who are more kinesthetic or intuitive usually prefer other strategies.

Value or learning style differences are neither right nor wrong, good nor bad. Some clients and financial professionals prefer certain approaches to others because of their individual style of learning. Given these differences, it is important for the financial professional to be able to adapt a variety of strategies to both the needs and the learning styles of various clients.

This chapter will present several decision making and problem solving strategies. You should be able to use each, as appropriate, in the manner presented. In addition, you should be able to understand the underlying concepts so that you can adapt, change, or combine various elements to fit the needs and learning styles of particular clients.

Framework. We have used both terms, decision making and problem solving, to refer to a set of strategies that can be used to help clients achieve goals. Theoretically, there is a distinction between the two. However, the strategies are alike. On a practical level we can say that decision making strategies are used when plans and procedures are needed to achieve specific goals. Problem solving strategies are used when we encounter an obstacle that prevents us from achieving our goals. Problem solving focuses on how to remove or circumvent obstacles.

Effectiveness of decision making and problem solving strategies usually is determined by the degree to which they help achieve specific goals. If the desired goal is reached, we probably would judge the strategy to be effective. If it fails to help us accomplish our goals, we are likely to judge it as ineffective. For example, if two people invest equal amounts of money, using identical decision making processes, and one person doubles his or her money while the other loses, the first person is likely to judge the decision making strategy as *good*, while the second person is likely to judge the strategy as *bad*. Neither judgment is necessarily true.

The *process* of decision making or problem solving must be separated from the *outcome*. Many things in the financial world that can affect outcomes are beyond your or the client's control. Effective decision making and problem solving strategies are designed to take into account as many contingencies as possible, recognizing that it is impossible to account for them all. There is always an element of luck or chance that can affect outcomes.

A major problem with judging strategies on the basis of outcomes is that if a strategy doesn't produce the desired results in one situation, it will be dismissed in other situations for which it might be highly appropriate. On the other hand, if a strategy is successful in achieving goals, it may be used inappropriately in another situation. Keep in mind that the value of decision making and problem solving strategies is determined by what they can be used to accomplish and that at different times, with different needs or goals, alternative strategies may be most appropriate.

Methods. People use a number of decision making and problem solving methods to achieve goals or to remove obstacles. Dilley (1970) outlines seven basic methods: (1) follow an accepted rule, (2) utilize a rational process, (3) act to gain social approval, (4) follow intuition, (5) leave it to fate or chance, (6) arrange a compromise, and (7) consult an expert. When people need to make a decision or to solve a problem, they subconsciously use one or more of these methods. An understanding of the natural decision making and problem solving processes clients might use can provide a basis for helping clients to make effective financial decisions or to solve financial problems. Each of the seven methods is described below. Keep in mind that while they are separated for discussion, they can be used in various combinations.

▸*Following an Accepted Rule*. People often make decisions by applying what they consider to be a relevant rule to the situation. They may apply the first rule that comes to mind or review several rules and apply the one that seems to have the greatest power in the specific situation. Clients can develop financial problems by following accepted rules, rules that have become part of our culture or that have been promulgated by advertising to benefit certain industries. Some commonly used "rules" are:

- Buy now, pay later.
- You don't have to wait until you have cash.
- Use your credit. You need a good credit rating.
- Buying on credit allows you to deduct interest and then pay for things with inflated dollars.
- As long as you make the minimum payment each month you will keep your credit rating.
- Travel now, pay later.
- Buy low, sell high.
- Don't put all your eggs into one basket. Develop a broad-based portfolio.

Such "rules" are designed to make complicated situations sound simple. Following an accepted rule works well in situations that repeat themselves regularly. One of the major limitations of following an accepted rule as a decision making or problem solving method is that there may be conflicting rules which apply to the same situation and then one is left with trying to decide which is most appropriate. For example, "Leverage your money" and "You can get the best deals if you pay cash" could both be good advice. However, they directly contradict each other in some situations. A second major problem with following an accepted rule is that people often use them as mandates rather than as guidelines. Therefore, you should help clients to become aware of the positive aspects of their rules while cautioning them against potential negative consequences. The difficulty is not in the rules, but rather in the inappropriate use of them.

▸*Utilizing a Rational Process*. There are a number of rational decision making or problem solving strategies. The underlying purpose in using a rational process is to predict possible consequences of various choices or actions. Through the examination of possible consequences, people attempt to narrow their choices to those that have the greatest potential for positive outcomes and the least potential for negative outcomes. Clients frequently make financial decisions based on their feelings or needs rather than on logical evaluation of information. When clients make decisions that are based on primary needs such as the need for security or status, you may fail to understand their motivation and wonder why they are not more logical in their choice of options. A valuable service that you can provide clients is to encourage them to identify their needs, help them to understand how their needs relate to their financial goals, and teach them to understand the value of rational decision making and problem solving strategies. A number of such strategies will be described later in this chapter.

▸ *Acting to Gain Social Approval*. In using this method, clients attempt to determine what people they admire value and then to make decisions that are consistent with those values. The old phrase "Keeping up with the Joneses" is an example of how individuals attempt to conform to attitudes, beliefs, or values of others, and how external influence is subtle yet powerful. Individuals are influenced both subtly and openly to do "as others are doing." One way financial professionals can use knowledge of this process with clients is by using *expert* opinions as a means of generating possible plans of action.

As a financial professional you often rely on the considered opinions of experts for financial information and investment strategies. While this use of expert opinion is one way of helping clients to make decisions or to solve problems, clients must remember that they are ultimately responsible for whatever decisions they make. Expert opinions never guarantee results. In the final analysis, clients must consider the information from relevant sources and then make their own decisions.

▸ *Following Intuition*. People often act without thinking things through completely. Impulsive buying is an example. A number of sayings or "rules" caution against impulsive or intuitive type buying, "Never shop when you're hungry," "Look before you leap," "Do you really need it?," "Don't buy it just because it is a bargain," and so on. People also make decisions based on their hunches or feelings. Good poker players often explain their success by saying that they have good hunches. Intuition or hunches are often based on subconscious information, information that is learned over time and leads to the "feeling" that one choice may be better than another in a given situation. Intuitive decision making or problem solving often appears to be impulsive, but may in fact be based on solid subconscious information.

There are two things to keep in mind about intuitive decision making or problem solving. First, people often buy or impulsively invest in a manner that can eventually cause financial problems. It is not that intuitive, impulsive buying is wrong. Rather, when a *pattern* of impulsive buying develops, a financial problem is more likely to occur. Of course, it will be a problem only if the results of impulsive actions are negative. If, for example, someone invests in the stock market, using "hunches" as an investment strategy, and continues to make money, who is to say it's wrong? Most of us, however, would say that they are lucky and would predict that in time their hunches will catch up with them.

Second, intuitive, creative thought usually doesn't occur without days, months, and even years of hard work. Intuitive, creative decisions that produce good results usually are based on a substantial amount of previously obtained information, much of which may be subconscious. Experience, especially financial experience, increases the probability that intuitive decision making or problem solving will produce positive results. Don't dismiss your intuition or that of your clients. The combination of intuitive and rational methods may increase the probability of generating positive outcomes because two complementary processes are incorporated.

▸*Leaving it to Fate or Chance.* Any process that involves chance (roll of the die, astrological reading, palm reading, etc.), luck, or accident belongs in this category. In addition, processes that involve using data that has no known logical connection with the issue at hand also fit this category. People who use their social security number, or the numeric representation of their birth date, or the car's serial number as a basis for buying lottery tickets are relying on fate or chance.

Leaving things to fate is often used by people to solve all kinds of problems. The old saying "Leave it alone and maybe it will go away" exemplifies this kind of decision making. People often hope that if they ignore things long enough fate or chance will cure everything. Professional financial relationships are, of course, based on assumptions directly contrary to this method of decision making or problem solving. As a financial professional, you should help clients become aware of the potential difficulties that can arise from leaving their financial lives to fate or chance.

▸ *Arranging a Compromise*. Arranging a compromise is a process that benefits at least two different people or that incorporates aspects of two different processes. In order to compromise, all involved parties must give up something. If one party is not willing to compromise, then a different form of conflict resolution must be used. Arranging a compromise is often an integral part of a professional financial relationship. This is especially true when working with couples.

▸ *Consulting an Expert*. When people come to you as a financial professional they are generally using the method of consulting an expert. They see you as having more information, more experience, and a better understanding of the financial world than they possess. Their expectation may be that, because of your expertise, you will be able to make decisions for them. Consequently, you are obligated to define your role early in your relationship, to share with your clients your perceived areas of expertise, to alert clients to referral sources you are accustomed to using, and to discuss decisions that you can and cannot make in the clients' behalf. The major danger with clients that choose to "consult an expert" is that they may expect you to make decisions for them. This may be appropriate in situations where you are the executor of an estate or a trust fund. However, in most situations, it is inappropriate to take responsibility for making clients' decisions. It is not inappropriate, however, to use your expertise to generate alternatives from which clients can make choices.

The seven decision making and problem solving approaches discussed above describe how people attempt to deal with their finances. No one method is better than the others in all situations. Methods can be combined to produce many ways people can make decisions and solve problems. An implicit goal in most professional financial relationships is to help people to make their own decisions and to solve their own problems. In this sense, you should become an expert in decision making and problem solving processes. One of the most valuable things you have to offer clients is the very process you use to help them. The anonymous quote, "If I give you a fish, I have fed you today. If I teach you how to fish I have fed you for a lifetime" attests to teaching clients a process that will make them more effective in their own right. To do this, you should become conversant with as many different decision making and problem solving processes as possible.

Two major classifications of decision making and problem solving methods are important in professional financial relationships: rational or logical strategies and intuitive or creative strategies. These two classifications correspond to the way our brain's hemispheres process information. The left hemisphere tends to process information in logical, step-by-step, rational ways. By contrast, the right hemisphere tends to be more intuitive, feeling, and holistic. Remember, however, that the hemispheres do not operate in an isolated fashion, so that while we may be approaching a problem or decision in a very rational manner, our intuition and feelings are still operative and affect what we do. The following are strategies that reflect differences in hemispheric functioning. Keep in mind, however, that in most financial situations the best strategy is an integrated one, one that uses aspects of both hemispheres.

Rational Decision Making and Problem Solving. The key to most rational methods is that they follow a sequential or step-by-step format. As clients logically and sequentially move through the steps there is a progressive narrowing to a decision or solution that can be applied to the situation. We will present four such rational methods: (1) Go/No-Go, (2) Problem Solving, (3) Decision Making, and (4) Time Zero.

▸*Go/No-Go*. The Go/No-Go decision making process has five steps, which are used after the person has determined what needs to be decided. It is especially useful in situations where a person is deciding on making a purchase. The steps are:

- Define absolutes
- Define nice-to-haves
- Predict the future by examining the past
- Eliminate nice-to-haves and adjust absolutes
- Go with the best balanced choice

For example, Mary, a realtor, was helping a client to purchase a new house. She asked her client to list all the features that the new purchase *must* have for it to be considered for purchase. In addition, Mary asked her client to elaborate on any additional features that would make the purchase of the house more attractive. At this point, Mary helped her client to examine both lists of features, those that were considered by the client to be absolutely necessary and those that would be "nice to have" but not mandatory. Mary asked her client to examine each feature and to project how frequently the feature would be used. To help her client to do this, Mary said, "One of the best ways to determine how often something will be used in the future is to look backward in time and to ask yourself, 'If I had that in the past, how often would I have used it?'" By getting her client to look backward, Mary provided a means for helping her client to understand what *probably* would happen in the future. Information gained in this manner was then used to help the client to eliminate alternatives that seemed to be needed but probably would be little used. Through this approach, Mary could help her client to make a balanced choice, one that reflected needs and wants while eliminating alternatives that might be "nice" but not necessary.

▸*Problem Solving.* The problem solving process outlined below incorporates six logical steps but also utilizes right hemispheric processes which rely on intuition.

- Identify a need (or needs)
- Establish a goal (or goals)
- Examine resources
- Brainstorm possible solutions
- Do not censor
- Do not clarify
- Do not assign names
- Use other people's ideas
- Select a solution or combination of solutions
- Evaluate in light of needs and goals

As an example of this strategy, consider Dana, who went to her financial planner for help in the development of an investment program. Dana's financial planner asked Dana what she hoped to accomplish through an investment program. As a result of the ensuing discussion, Dana realized that she was most interested in preparing for an early retirement and, consequently, she established a goal of having $200,000 committed to investments in the next fifteen-year period.

Dana's financial planner helped Dana to use this long-term goal to establish intermediate goals and then helped Dana to examine all of her financial resources that would be used to achieve both sets of goals. In this discussion, the financial planner focused on monetary assets such as wages, savings, investments, and financial inheritances as well as on personal resources such as motivation, commitment, and willingness to take risks.

Once Dana and the financial planner had discussed these resources in detail, the financial planner helped Dana to *brainstorm* all possible means for Dana to reach her financial goals. This led Dana to consider many ideas, some of which had potential merit, some of which did not. Of the many ideas that were generated, Dana was able to select an investment strategy that allowed her to invest on a regular basis, in a manner that maximized her chances of reaching both her intermediate and long-term goals.

Finally, Dana's financial planner established a systematic means for assessing, on a periodic basis, the degree to which Dana was meeting her goals. This provided Dana a way for working toward her goals *and* the flexibility to adjust to a changing financial climate.

▸*Decision Making*. The rational decision making process described below incorporates steps and concepts from several other methods that have been found to be effective. As with the methods described above, there are logical steps designed to help the client to make the best balanced decision.

- Examine needs
- Establish goals
- Generate alternative solutions
- Estimate the costs of each solution in terms of money, emotions, time, effort, social relations, etc.
- Outline the benefits of each solution.
- Determine the likelihood of success for each solution.
- Consider the seriousness of failure of each solution.
- Set a game plan for each solution: If accepted,*who* will do *what, when*, and *where*?

The strength of this strategy lies in its ability to provide a systematic examination of alternatives. The example that follows demonstrates how this strategy can be applied to a financial concern.

Kelvin inherited $100,000, which he wished to invest. In thinking about possible investments, Kelvin was aware that he had a need for security and, yet, that he was willing to take moderate risks so that his money would grow faster than the rate of inflation. With this in mind, Kelvin began to actively think about ways to achieve his financial goal. He generated a number of alternatives. Some would meet his goal of staying ahead of inflation, whereas others would not. Some entailed high risk, others were relatively risk free. To be systematic in his approach, Kelvin decided to examine all alternatives by applying the strategy presented above.

One of the alternatives that Kelvin considered was to invest his money in a multiple-unit apartment building. It became apparent to Kelvin that this alternative would have a number of *costs*. In addition to the obvious *financial* costs for a down payment, closing costs, legal fees, insurance outlays, etc. Kelvin became aware of the amount of *time* he might have to commit to overseeing this investment, the *effort* he might have to expend to assure that the investment would be productive, and the *worry* he might have about his undertaking.

Kelvin also became aware of the many potential *benefits* of this alternative: He realized that he probably would make an annual profit that would exceed the annual rate of inflation; that his investment, if properly maintained, would increase in value; that he would feel good about owning a multiple unit; and that his investment would be relatively risk free.

Kelvin then rated his chances of being successful with this alternative on a 10-point scale, with "10" being a high degree of success, and determined that his chances of success would be about "nine out of ten."

Kelvin then decided how serious failure would be. He determined, on a 10-point scale in which 10 would be very serious, that failure on this alternative would be quite serious to his long-term financial plans and, therefore, rated failure as a potential "10."

Kelvin did not set a game plan for this alternative because he wanted to find a more ideal alternative, one that had "a high likelihood of success" and a low "seriousness of failure."

Kelvin then repeated this process for all of the solutions he had generated. Once he settled on an alternative, he would make decisions about *who* would do *what, when*, and *where* to initiate action on the chosen alternative.

▶ *Time Zero.* The Time Zero problem solving approach was developed by John P. Decker (1978) at Arizona State University as a rational approach for dealing with personality clashes or conflicts. This method has been taught to engineers and other professionals who are in supervisory positions and who are called on to resolve personality clashes. The method is based on an assumption that nearly all personality conflicts between people follow the same basic pattern. Once the basic pattern is recognized, the problem solving steps can be used to bring about resolution. We think the method may be important for financial professionals in several ways: (1) dealing with employees, (2) dealing with fellow professionals, and (3) helping clients resolve interpersonal conflicts.

When interpersonal conflicts arise, a high degree of emotionality usually is involved. People became angry and feel hurt, depressed, or confused. As they attempt to deal with their feelings there is a tendency to look for excuses to justify how they feel. Once strong emotions are activated, people tend to overgeneralize and to blame others.

The first step in the Time Zero problem solving method is to identify common errors that people exhibit when they become emotionally aroused. The common errors are defined in the box (see page 166).

Time Zero problem solving methods revolve around accurately diagnosing the situation. As you listen to your client, who is in a conflict situation, you attempt to identify each of the common errors outlined above. This can provide you a better understanding of your client and some understanding of the situation. Keep in mind, however, that the four common errors are not produced in all conflict situations. There may be times that clients will define their problem in a faulty way and move directly to some form of impulsive solution without going through, on a conscious level, the blaming involved in the impulsive explanation. Thus, when a client or colleague brings an interpersonal conflict to you, there is potential for any or all of the common errors. After you have listened to or elicited the person's explanations, you can use the six-step process to help him or her resolve the problem.

▸ *Calm the person.* People usually are in an emotional state when they seek help. Good problem solving involves some form of reasoning. Yet, it may be difficult to be logical when strong emotions are being exhibited. A productive approach to reduce emotional responses and to calm aroused individuals is to verbally pace the person by restating or paraphrasing at the emotional or theme level. Verbal pacing at the emotional level communicates that you accept the individual's emotions and are willing to deal with them.

Time Zero—Common Errors

▶ *Faulty statement of the problem.* People tend to make faulty statements of their problem in one of two ways. The first is to use imprecise words to express both the existence of a problem and to express their feelings. For example, "I'm in trouble with John now" or "I've really got a problem" are statements which express strong feelings but lack any reference to what the problem might be. The second "faulty" reaction is to overgeneralize from the conflict situation. That is, people often use a single conflict situation to make general judgments about their relationships with other people. For example, after getting into an argument about how to invest, one spouse might overgeneralize by saying something like, "He never listens to me and what I want to do. He just bulldozes me into what he wants to do." In this case, the client is expressing a strong feeling and in the process has generalized to every experience of discussing investments. People usually generalize to justify their strong feelings.

▶ *Impulsive explanation.* Another way in which people attempt to justify their strong feelings is to place the responsibility for their feelings on others. When people do this, it appears that they are saying that they have a right to feel as they do because others did something that *made* them angry, frustrated, or hurt. Usually, inherent in these forms of explanations is some negative judgment about either the character or the behavior of others. Returning to the previous example, the spouse might give an impulsive explanation such as, "He is just so pushy all the time. He thinks he knows everything and thinks that, as a woman, I'm just dumb when it comes to managing money." Notice that the explanation revolves around making negative judgments about both the character of the spouse and assumptions about the way he thinks about her. Again, the primary purpose is to blame the other person for the feelings that were activated during the conflict.

▶ *Impulsive solution.* When conflicts arise, the natural tendency is to want to punish others. Having overgeneralized and blamed others for present feelings, people usually attempt some solution which will "get them even." The punishing and getting even is often self-defeating. That is, the solution of punishing others usually maintains the conflict, intensifies feelings, and often makes the original problem situation worse. Again, returning to the conflict between spouses, "I'll fix him. I'll just spend all my money on something I want, and I won't even discuss investing with him again." The impulsive solution becomes self-defeating in that the conflict may be intensified and the person is inhibiting herself from making wise investment decisions.

▶ *Plea for endorsement.* Pleas for endorsement take place in two ways. First, implicitly, through tone of voice and nonverbal behavior clients may ask you to agree with how they have defined the problem, with their impulsive explanation, or with their impulsive solution. Secondly, explicitly, clients may ask for your agreement. For example, "Isn't that right?" or "Don't you agree that it's a bad choice?" or "Isn't that what you would do?" It is important for you to recognize when clients are seeking your agreement so that you do not get forced into a position counter to your beliefs. Once you get forced into agreeing with how your clients defined the problem, accepting their impulsive explanation, or agreeing with their impulsive solution, you will have lost your ability to help them move to an alternative way of solving the problem.

Your purpose at this point is to calm the person so that the two of you can discuss on a more rational level what has happened.

▸ *Draw attention to the present moment and identify the trigger event.* The present moment is time zero, the beginning of the future. People often continue their emotional upset by reliving the past. The more they think about the past and what occurred, the more upset they become. This starts a negative cycle. The more upset they become, the more likely they are to relive old experiences. This, in turn, reinforces the feelings, and so on.

This negative cycle limits the ability to think rationally about the situation. People often project past experiences to future imagined encounters with others. They start to imagine future encounters occurring in the same manner as past encounters. This limits their ability to solve problems rationally. We can help people move to time zero by helping them to focus on the trigger event, the one thing that happened which led to the present emotional upset. Usually one or more stimuli bring on a strong emotional response. Your goal is to help the person identify the trigger event in the present conflict situation. For instance, you could ask your client, "What one specific thing happened that led to your present feelings?"

▸ *Help the person decide what he or she wants to happen next.* In this step, the person moves toward establishing goals. The goals should relate specifically to the conflict situation and to the trigger event. Such goals are most easily stated in terms of what the person wants to happen in future encounters with others. In the example above, you might ask the spouse, "What do you want to happen when you talk to your husband about investing?" The client might respond, "I want him to listen to me. I want him to recognize that I have some good ideas too!" At this point, you have successfully moved the client to the present, time zero. You have identified the trigger event and have helped the client decide what is desired in the future.

▸ *Help the person develop a plan.* The plan will vary with the type of conflict, but it often will focus on how the person can respond in future potential conflict situations. In our example above, it might include deciding specifically what the person might say when the next trigger event occurs. For example, "The next time your husband acts that way, what do you think you could do differently?" The client might respond, "Well, I guess I could tell him how I'm feeling." The financial professional might respond, "What specifically would you say?" At this point, the goal is to develop specific steps which can be thought through and even rehearsed as preparation for future interactions.

In other conflict situations the plan may focus on specific steps similar to those we develop to accomplish other types of goals, such as developing a marketing plan or a sales plan. The emphasis should be on specifics—*who* is going to do *what, when*, and *where*? It may also be constructive during this step to help the person compare the new plan of action with the old, impulsive process that fostered the conflict.

▸ *Help the person to become self-monitoring*. One of the most valuable things we can do for clients is to teach them the very process we used to help them. Of course, this is done implicitly when we use a method such as the Time Zero approach. However, we cannot assume that just because people experience a process they have learned it. The method used with a client in one situation probably will be helpful to the client in similar future situations. But, we should also be concerned about people learning to utilize the method in other conflict situations. This is most easily done by discussing with the client the steps you have used and how they might be used in other conflict situations.

In all of the rational decision making and problem solving approaches described above, the emphasis has been on logical thinking. Sequential steps help people to do that. Common to all of the approaches is the stating of goals, the orderly generation of alternatives, and the evaluation of possible solutions. The methods vary in the emphasis they place on kinds and forms of information they use to arrive at meaningful solutions. The difficulty with most rational approaches is not in the methods or processes, but in the people who use them. It is difficult to stay on a purely logical or rational level. We each have values, attitudes, beliefs, and feelings which, at times, sidestep our logic. The old saying "Don't confuse me with the facts. My mind is already made up!" exemplifies how values, attitudes, beliefs, and feelings can defy logical, rational thinking. Rational problem solving and decision making also take effort and time. Often we prefer to do what comes naturally or intuitively. This is not to say that rational approaches are not powerful processes. People would probably make better decisions in their lives if they were more rational, but there are other ways of decision making and problem solving that are used. These other forms can be classified as being right hemispheric or intuitive methods.

Intuitive and Creative Approaches. Rational decision making and problem solving approaches proceed in a stepwise fashion, with each step forming the basis for the next step. You cannot start in the middle because the foundations of the previous steps have not been laid. You start from what you know and go straight ahead, following the steps sequentially. For the outcome of rational processes to be effective, each step in the process must produce desired results. Rational approaches are highly esteemed, and rightly so. However, they are not the only way of arriving at solutions.

At times, people have "bright ideas" that seem to pop into their heads and that frequently seem to work. Whenever solutions are generated in this intuitive or creative way, you can usually see in hindsight how they could have been arrived at by rational processes. This usually is true, or the solution wouldn't be acceptable or produce the desired effects. In rational methods, we usually begin with certain psychological sets about the problem or situation. These sets then guide our logic and are used as a basis for evaluating both information and the steps used. Intuitive or creative decision making and problem solving, however, often disregard previous psychological sets or, at least, uses different ones. It may sound like a contradiction to have intuitive or creative problem solving methods because they just seem to happen in our experience. The usual intuitive or creative methods are aimed at blocking our use of subconscious psychological sets and at forcing us to think about the decision or problem differently. They encourage free thinking. While there are a large number of these intuitive or creative methods we will describe only six of them: Brainstorming, Problem Expansion, Problem Reversal, Using a Random Stimulus, Making It Worse, and Using a Solution to One Problem to Solve Another.

Brainstorming. Brainstorming is a process of free association. It can be used by an individual but is more productive when used by two or more people. The basic premise of this approach is that ideas stimulate other ideas. Consequently, the general process of brainstorming involves saying or writing down all ideas or thoughts about a problem that come to mind. Ideas generated in this manner may, in turn, stimulate further ideas or thoughts. Keep in mind the following "rules" for brainstorming.

▸*Do not censor*. The purpose of brainstorming is to generate as many ideas as possible. Yet, people have a natural tendency to evaluate their ideas before they voice them or write them down.

Their self-evaluation is often negative. They might think that the idea would never work in the given situation and, therefore, they tend not to share it. By avoiding the censoring process, individuals can say whatever comes to mind, no matter how relevant they think it might be. Ideas generated in this manner could stimulate others' thoughts about alternatives for the given concern.

▶ *Do not clarify*. Do not spend time explaining ideas or concepts. Clarifying has a tendency to slow down new idea generation. The purpose of brainstorming is to generate as many ideas as possible.

▶ *Do not assign names*. If brainstorming is used with two or more people, there may be an inclination to assign names to specific ideas, i.e., Joe came up with idea X, Mary had idea Y, or Cindy thought of idea Z. Assigning names often slows down idea generation and limits the free reaction to an idea at later stages of brainstorming.

▶ *Use other people's ideas*. Since the brainstorming process uses all available stimuli for generating ideas, one person's ideas or thoughts may stimulate another's ideas or thoughts. Consider the following as an example of this process.

Financial professional: Well, Kathy, what thoughts have you had about obtaining additional insurance coverage?

Kathy: I've been thinking of some of the benefits, but so far I've only come up with the security it provides.

Financial professional: Do you mean security from worry? . . . or security from claims against you? . . . or something else?

Kathy: I guess I was just thinking about personal security, but your questions make me think about a number of other things I should consider, like how insurance provides me more than just security.

Financial professional: That's good. Let's brainstorm some of the things that insurance can provide, besides security.

In this example, the financial professional initially used the brainstorming process informally. In the financial professional's last statement you can see a movement toward a formal use of the technique.

Brainstorming encourages free association and thus breaks previously held assumptions and attitudes. The process encourages the generation of a great number of possible solutions that subsequently can be evaluated on the basis of problem relevancy and potential effectiveness.

Problem Expansion. The problem expansion method combines two steps to help you get away from standard ways of thinking. The first step is to repeatedly define what you think the problem is. The second step requires that you use the brainstorming process to generate solutions for how you defined the problem each time. The problem expansion process can be used through a number of cycles, a cycle being the process of defining the problem and brainstorming solutions.

This process is usually most effective if used through at least three cycles. That is, (1) define the problem and brainstorm solutions, (2) redefine the problem and brainstorm solutions, (3) again redefine the problem and brainstorm solutions. Very often people discover that no matter how they define the problem, similar solutions get generated in each brainstorming session. This may be the hallmark of a good solution, one that applies no matter how the problem is defined. Following are two examples, one to highlight the process and another to illustrate how this technique might be applied to a financial decision making or problem solving situation.

Suppose you are driving to an important meeting. Suppose, as well, that you have allowed yourself just enough time to get to the meeting with a few minutes to spare. While driving to the meeting, you discover you have a flat tire. When you look in the trunk for the jack and the spare tire, you notice the jack is broken.

Given the situation as stated, how would you define the problem? The way you define the problem will affect the kinds of solutions you generate. If you define the problem as getting to the meeting on time, you might call a cab, you might hitchhike, or you might call someone you know to come and get you. If you define the problem as one of changing the tire, you might flag another motorist down to borrow a jack, you might call a service station to have someone come and fix the flat, or you might drive the car on the flat tire to the nearest service station to have the tire changed. If you define the problem as a broken jack, you might try to fix the jack, you might, again, flag down a passing motorist to borrow a jack; or you might find some other way of lifting the car so that you can change the tire without a jack, such as driving the car so that the flat tire is sitting in a deep hole or hanging over the edge of the road. Notice that each time you define the problem differently, different solutions come to mind. Let's apply this technique to a financial example.

Financial professional: Good morning, Ned. What brings you in today?

Ned: Good morning. I think I'm really stuck . . .

Financial professional: What seems to be the problem?

Ned: I'm having trouble meeting all of my expenses . . . I don't seem to have enough money to go around.

Financial professional: Okay . . . we can attack this in a number of ways . . . let's just generate some ideas . . . is that all right with you?

Ned: That sounds good to me.

Financial professional: Could it be that you don't have enough income?

Ned: I suppose so.

Financial professional: How might you generate more income?

Ned: I could up the rent on my apartment units, or I could work more hours at my part-time job, or I could even get a full-time job.

Financial professional: All of those sound like possibilities. Another way to look at your problem might be to cut down on your expenses . . . how might you do that?

Ned: That's a good idea . . . I could do more around the apartments myself instead of paying others to do every little thing . . . or I could see if I could get a better deal on some of the things I've been buying for the apartments . . .

Financial professional: Excellent ideas . . . now, let's switch the focus one more time. What besides income and expenses might be causing you to feel short of money?

Ned: I think that I've been pretty loose lately . . . I've bought whatever I've wanted when I wanted it. I could just be more careful and get my family to do the same.

Financial professional: It does sound as though there are a number of things that you could do to get over the difficulty you're in. Where would you like to begin?

Problem expansion forces us to break our initial way of thinking about the problem or decision making situation by forcing us to redefine a number of times. Each new definition will lead to a new set of solutions. Remember, if the same solutions seem to be generated no matter how you define the problem, you probably have several solutions that could be effective.

Problem Reversal. Problem reversal, like other intuitive or creative methods, forces us to examine the decision or problem situation from a new or different perspective. To do this, you turn the decision or problem situation around and approach it from the end rather than from the beginning. A simple example will illustrate the process.

Suppose you were asked to organize a community singles tennis tournament. One hundred people signed up for the single elimination tournament. The problem you are faced with is to determine how many matches will be needed to complete the competition. The natural, logical way most people would solve this problem is to lay out a tournament sheet. You would start with 50 matches from which there would be 50 winners. These 50 winners would then be paired for a second round of matches, and there would then be 25 new winners. At this point, there would have been 75 matches. You would proceed, logically, until you discovered how many matches you would need to declare a champion of the tournament.

Had you started at the end (problem reversal), however, you could have arrived at the answer much more quickly. The champion must win all matches and everyone else must lose. That means that we need as many matches as there are people . . . less the one, the person who always wins. That means that we need 99 matches in the tournament. When you read the solution it makes logical sense, but notice that it was determined by proceeding in an intuitive, nonsequential manner. This same method can be applied in some financial situations. Consider Jane's interaction with her realtor, Gloria.

Gloria: Jane, you've been trying to get a down payment together for some time now. How are you doing?

Jane: Not very well. I keep adding to my collection of antique glass and don't seem to have money left over for anything else. I've thought about not collecting for a while, but I truly enjoy the pieces and the process of collecting them. I'm not sure I'll ever have enough money for a down payment on a house!

Gloria: Maybe you already have what you need . . . you might be able to use your antiques collection as collateral for a down payment loan.

Jane: Is that right? . . . I've been trying to think of ways of coming up with the money and it may have been right in front of me all the time!

In this interchange, Gloria was able to *reverse* the problem by viewing Jane's antique glass collection as a form of savings rather than as a drain on revenue. This intuitive perspective could provide Jane an alternative that could lead to solution of her problem.

Using a Random Stimulus. Intuitive or creative decision making and problem solving methods help break our normal attitudes and assumptions. Using a random stimulus forces us to do that. Using a random stimulus suggests that we utilize something which, on the surface, doesn't appear to apply to our decision or problem situation as a basis for generating new solutions. The most common random stimulus used is a word chosen randomly from a dictionary or a book.

The book is opened at random to any page, and a word is randomly selected. The randomly selected word is used as a stimulus for brainstorming possible solutions. For example, one of the authors was working with a group of credit union managers, one of whom mentioned that a major problem in the credit union was dealing with a large number of customers at peak hours. The customers would stand in long lines and become impatient while waiting their turn. The customers would then take their impatience out on the tellers. A number of solutions had been tried, but none seemed to solve the problems. As a group, the credit union managers were asked to use the random stimulus method to try to generate possible solutions. One of the managers had a book about Mexico with her. The author asked a manager to randomly open the book. He then had another manager point randomly to a word on the page. The word pointed to was *fiesta*, the Spanish word for a party. The group was then asked to brainstorm possible solutions by applying the word *fiesta* to the problem of long lines of customers. The group generated solutions similar to the following.

- Make it a party.
- Give out balloons.
- Give a prize to the person who had to wait the longest.
- Serve refreshments while people wait.
- Play video cartoons for the children in one area of the lobby to keep them happy and occupied.
- Have "theme" nights, when the tellers would dress up differently, in Mexican, Hawaiian, or Indian costume, for example.
- Play music.
- Have customers take a number and then go for refreshments or watch television until their number was called.
- Greet the people at the door and give them a party favor for coming in on a busy night.

The manager later reported to the author that several of the ideas that had been generated using the random stimulus were combined and tried. The result was that the customers expressed appreciation for the thoughtfulness. The customers were less likely to be angry and impatient with the tellers, and the tellers seemed to be able to keep their composure and respond to the customers in more helpful and pleasant ways.

Making It Worse. One characteristic of problems is that when they are unresolved they tend to get worse. Making it worse is an intuitive or creative process that utilizes this concept by amplifying it. In effect, it begins with the question, "How can I possibly make the problem worse?" or "What can I do to make sure we have the worst possible outcome?" Once you have decided how you can make the problem worse or how you can guarantee that you will get the worst possible outcome, the focus is shifted to how you can use this perspective to solve the problem.

An example from industry: A chemical manufacturer situated in a northern state was having trouble with the reservoir water pumping system. The water, used as a coolant during the manufacturing process, was pumped continuously from and to the reservoir. The pumping station was located in the center of the reservoir, at its deepest point. During the winter the water would freeze and, at times, the pump in the station would also freeze. When the pumping station froze, the plant would shut down until the pump could be repaired. A number of different solutions had been tried, but none was entirely satisfactory.

Finally, one of the plant engineers arrived at a creative solution using the process of "making it worse." In answer to the question "What could you do to make sure the pump froze?" the engineer decided that the best way to accomplish that would be to pump liquid nitrogen into the pumping station. Liquid nitrogen is used to make dry ice. It freezes very quickly. If liquid nitrogen were pumped into the station, it would freeze into a solid block of ice. If that could be used to make sure the worst possible outcome was achieved, how could it be used to solve the problem? The engineer responded that you could probably pump something else into the station that wouldn't freeze—antifreeze! The solution, then, became very simple. When the cold weather began and there was a danger of the pump freezing, the engineer simply filled the station with antifreeze. The plant no longer had to stop manufacturing because of a frozen pump.

The process of "making it worse" can also be applied to financial situations. Consider the following:

Marion was having difficulty knowing where his money was going. It seemed to him that he should be able to save on a regular basis and, yet, at the end of each month he felt financially "strapped" and unable to save. When Marion asked himself "What would make my situation worse?" he decided that if he had $100 less in monthly income he would experience financial difficulty. To test this idea, Marion decided to place $100 in the bank at the *beginning* of the month and to use this sum only for emergency purposes. Marion discovered that he was able to do what he wanted to do during the month and that he ended the month with no greater financial difficulty than he had before he started setting the $100 aside. After experimenting with "making it worse" by setting aside $100, Marion decided that he could make it on $100 less in spending money and, therefore, to use this approach as a regular form of savings.

Using a Solution to One Problem to Solve Another. There are times that we find solutions to problems by using rational or an intuitive/creative means. These solutions, or achievement of desired outcomes in one situation, can sometimes provide a stimulus or means for determining solutions in other situations. In mathematics, for example, frequently a final solution is determined by solving a series of interrelated problems in which the final answer is dependent on answers to subsequent steps. This process also has uses in the financial realm. The following examples demonstrate how this can occur.

Example 1: Ellen wanted to purchase a new automobile without using her savings. To do this, she had to find a way of coming up with a sufficient down payment. When faced with similar situations in the past, Ellen had asked her parents for the money needed and then paid them back out of her regular earnings. She again considered this possibility, but decided that she would rather find another source of funding. Ellen thought about the *solution* she had previously used, which stimulated her to think of how she could borrow to provide a down payment for her automobile. This process eventually led Ellen to consider borrowing against her life insurance policy as a source of funding.

Example 2: Rod wanted to build a new house. In order to obtain a construction mortgage, he had to have a 10% down payment or proof that he owned the property on which the house was to be built. Rod therefore decided to achieve his long-term goal of building the house by first achieving his short-term goal, owning the land on which the house was to be built. To accomplish this short-term goal, Rod reflected on how in the past he used equity in his house as collateral for obtaining a home improvement loan. Consequently, Rod decided to purchase the land that the new house was to be built on and to use it as collateral for obtaining a construction mortgage.

In the first of these examples, Ellen used the solution from previous financial problems as a *stimulus* for her present problem. By contrast, Rod used the solution of buying the property as a *means* for solving his long-term goal.

In conclusion, decision making and problem solving can employ both logical, rational, orderly strategies *and* intuitive reasoning to arrive at meaningful solutions. It should be clear that situations differ and that the process used in one situation may or may not be appropriate in another. As you communicate with your clients you will be expected to determine which strategy is best in a given situation. Your understanding of communication and decision making and problem solving will provide the basis on which you will be able to make decisions that will be helpful to your clients.

Postscript

Communication Principles in Practice

Bob and Pat have made an appointment to meet with a financial planner, Mary, to talk about planning and preparing for their children's future education. Mary's office is a corner office on the second floor of a commercial office building. The office is average-sized, with a desk and several chairs situated so that Mary and clients can enjoy the pastoral view from the windows. In the corner of the office is a small seating arrangement of a couch, corner table with lamp, a small coffee table, and several comfortable chairs. The office is painted off-white, the desk and tables are wood-stained in a neutral pecan finish, the chairs and couch are tan. There is a large plant in one corner. Mary has several large photographs of country scenes over the couch, and on the wall behind her desk are diplomas laminated on walnut backgrounds: her MBA diploma and her CFP (Certified Financial Professional) certificate. As the clients arrive, Mary greets them at the door and offers both a cup of coffee. Mary asks the secretary to bring coffee and then directs Bob and Pat to the corner seating arrangement.

Mary: It's good to see both of you again. How have you been?

Bob: I've been good . . . enjoying the summer and a little time off.

Pat: Me, too. So far this summer I've had a lot of time to relax and enjoy myself.

Mary: Great! It's good to hear that you are both feeling good and enjoying yourselves. . . . So, exactly what brings you in today?

Bob: Pat and I were talking it over last week and we suddenly realized that we only have three years until Jimmy, our oldest, will be going to college, and then three years later Betsy will be on her way—that is, if they both want to go to college.

Mary: It sounds like you don't think you have much time to get ready and then there will be at least one year that you will have two children in college at the same time. I'm wondering what kinds of things you might have already done to get ready for this.

Bob: Well, not a whole lot. You know we built that new home six years ago. We had just outgrown that little cracker box we were in . . . and . . . we wanted to move where the schools were better for the kids. We have been doing some systematic savings, that you helped us get started, but . . . well, you know . . . we'd hate to wipe out our savings to send the kids to college.

Mary: To get started, let's review your situation to make sure my files are up to date. What is your gross income now? (Mary, Bob, and Pat explore the details of the couple's present financial situation.)

Mary finds out that Bob's present net income is approximately $28,000 a year and that Pat has gone back to work full time as an elementary teacher with a net income of $22,000 a year. At this time Bob and Pat have moderate indebtedness—house payment, a car payment (Bob and Pat own two cars, but planned their car purchases so that they will have only one car payment at a time), and the usual running expenses. Their health insurance, including dental coverage, is paid for at Bob's place of employment. Previously, Mary had helped Bob convert his whole life insurance policy into a form of term insurance, and Bob and Pat have been investing the difference in premiums in a mutual fund on a monthly basis. The recent increase in their disposable income and its effect on their life style has been a welcome addition. The family has been able to take several trips that they couldn't afford previously. The only other investing Bob and Pat have done is for both of them to put the maximum into an IRA (when permitted by law) and to start a money market account at their local credit union.

Mary: "I think that brings me up to date. You said earlier that your primary concern was preparing for your children's college education.

Bob: From everything I've been reading in the paper, it is going to cost a bundle! Besides that, it looks like we will have two in college at the same time . . . at least for a year.

Pat: I think it's important to help the kids as much as possible. Without our parents' support neither one of us would have gone to college, and we would like to provide the same thing for our own kids. Our incomes will increase, but I don't think we can plan on much more than staying just a little ahead of the inflation rate.

Bob: As we've talked about it, it seems that we might be able to handle the additional expenses out of our monthly income. After all, we made it on one income for a long time, but we don't relish having to live that way again. I guess we have gotten kind of spoiled the last year or so with two incomes.

Mary: It's awful nice not to have to think about every nickel you spend, and now that you have a taste of a little better life style, you don't want to step backward. Tell me what you mean when you say that you want to provide the children with some college support.

Pat: Well, I would like to be able to give them money for tuition, books, basic housing, clothes, and a little spending money. Any of the extras like season tickets for sports, fraternity or sorority dues, the usual college trips with their friends, and stuff like that I think they should be able to cover.

Bob: It's not that we want to give them a free ride. We think college is hard enough without having to worry about money or working part-time to make it through. We expect them to find summer jobs to help with their own clothes and to cover the extras.

Mary: You want to be able to provide the basic educational support. What do you think it will run a year?

Bob: We have told the kids that we will try to cover the basic expenses equivalent to what it would cost for them to go to the state university. If they want to go out of state or to one of those fancy private colleges, we've told them, they will have to come up with the difference out of their own work or through scholarships and loans.

Mary: That sounds fair enough to me. How much does it cost now at State University?

Pat: I checked into that while I was completing my master's degree. With books, tuition, and dorm fees, it costs $1,800 a semester. When you add about $30 a month in spending money and clothes for the year, we figure it would cost about $4,500 a year if Jimmy were going to college this year.

Mary: That's at today's prices. If we figure, conservatively, an inflation rate of about 8% . . . let's see . . . you said Jimmy would be going to college in three years . . . that would be a 24% increase by then . . . that would mean that it will cost in the neighborhood of . . . $5500 a year by the time Jimmy goes to college.

Bob: Whew! There go any family vacations!

Mary: I don't want to sound too pessimistic about all this, but if we keep our conservative estimate of 8% a year inflation then it will cost . . . let's see . . . $6,800 the year Jimmy is a senior in college, and that will also be the year that Betsy will be starting. During that year you will be looking at total expenses somewhere around $13,600. Then you will have four more years with Betsy in college. Let me doing a little more figuring here . . . .(Mary turns to her calculator) . . . I'll just figure this in round figures. Figuring an average of $5,500 a year for Jimmy and $7,500 a year for Betsy, that would mean that you will have about $72,000 in expenses to provide your children with their college education.

Bob: Wow! I knew it would be expensive, but I never thought it out all the way to see what it would be. That means that if we saved every penny of Pat's income for the next three years we might just make it!

Mary: That's surely one way to think about. Earlier you said that you didn't want to return to your old life style of watching every nickel. If you do that, you might have to again.

Pat: You're right. It would be a lot nicer if we don't have to do that again, but the kids' education is really important to us.

Mary: I've had a number of clients with the same concern. Some have started a regular investment program in a stock portfolio where their best guess is that their investments will increase much faster than inflation. They let their money work for them, so that college expenses won't all have to come out of savings. Others have set up savings accounts for their children. However, new tax law changes will have to be considered here. That option has other dangers. The money is given to the children, and when they reach 18 they may decide to use it for something other than college. There are other possibilities.

Bob: Some of those sound interesting. We don't know very much about investing. The mutual funds we've been investing in with the insurance thing are really doing well. But I can't see myself playing the stock market.

Mary: When you say, 'I can't see myself playing the stock market,' what does that mean to you?

Bob: I guess I'm a little afraid of investing without a lot of knowledge, and I don't want to take the time to learn all I'd need to know.

Pat: The stock market is somewhat frightening to me.

Mary: One of my clients, in a situation is similar to yours, said to me, "You can make a lot of money in the market if you use professional management, but it sure is risky on your own." It seems to me that he had a good point and that you might agree with him. Would you?

Bob: Yeah, I do agree with him. Especially since I want to make sure that I have the money when I need it for my kids' education.

Mary: Our conversation has been helpful in providing me insight into your concerns. I can see that you are concerned about your kids' education and in maintaining your standard of living. It is also apparent that you would like to use money in a prudent manner. In general, you've thought about some possibilities and appear ready to take some action. Would you agree with this assessment?

Pat: I sure do. I want to get prepared for the next few years by making some good decisions real soon.

Bob: I agree.

Mary: Okay, to arrive at some possible choices we'll need some additional information. We both have some homework to do. I'll need certain information from you about your financial resources, and I have to research what financial possibilities might be best given your specific situation. Let's set a date for going over what we come up with. How would a week from today be?

Bob: A week from today at the same time sounds good to me.

Pat: Sure, I can be here.

Mary: Good—now let me tell you what information I'm going to need so that next week we can really dig into this.

Following this statement, Mary outlines the needed information and prepares Bob and Pat for the next meeting. While walking the couple to the door, Mary says, Thanks for coming in; it was good to talk with you both. In talking about your situation I was struck by how similar life is to playing a game like golf or tennis. In both cases, luck or chance can play a big part . . . yet, if you prepare yourself you *can* have a lot of control over your own destiny. I'll see you next week.

References and Additional Resources

Adams, J.L. *Conceptual Blockbusting: A Guide to Better Ideas.* New York: W.W. Norton and Co., 1979.

Assagioli, R. *The Act of Will.* Baltimore: Penguin Books, Inc., 1974.

Bandler, R., and J. Grinder. *The Structure of Magic,* Vol. I. Palo Alto, CA: Science & Behavior Books, Inc., 1975.

Bandler, R., and J. Grinder. *The Structure of Magic,* Vol. II. Palo Alto, CA: Science & Behavior Books, Inc., 1976.

Bandler, R., and J. Grinder. *Frogs into Princes. Neuro-Linguistic Programming.* Moab, UT: Real People Press, 1980.

Bandler, R., and J. Grinder. *Reframing: Neuro-Linguistic Programming & the Transformation of Meaning.* Moab, UT: Real People Press, 1982.

Benjamin, A.D. *The Helping Interview.* Boston: Houghton Mifflin Co., 1981.

Brammer, L. *The Helping Relationship. Process and Skills.* Englewood Cliffs, NJ.: Prentice-Hall, 1985.

Buscaglia, L. *Love.* Thorofare, NJ: Charles B. Slack, 1972.

Buscaglia, L. *Living, Loving and Learning.* New York: Fawcett Columbine, 1983.

Buzan, T. *Using Both Sides of Your Brain.* New York: E.P. Dutton, 1983.

Decker, John P. *Solving Personality Clashes With Time Zero.* Tempe, AZ: Synecology Press, 1978

Dilley, J. *Higher Education Participants Confronted.* Dubuque, IA: W.C. Brown Publishers, 1970.

Edwards, B. *Drawing on the Right Side of Your Brain.* Los Angeles, CA: J.P. Tarcher, 1979.

Eisenberg, S., and L. Patterson. *The Counseling Process.* Boston: Houghton Mifflin Co., 1982.

Erikson, M. *My Voice Will Go with You: The Teaching Tales of Milton H. Erikson, M.D.* New York: W.W. Norton and Co., 1982.

Evans, D.R., et al. *Essential Interviewing: A Programmed Approach to Effective Communication.* Monterey, CA: Brooks/Cole Publishing Co., 1983.

Filley, A.C. *Interpersonal Conflict Resolution.* Glenview, IL: Scott Foresman, 1975.

Fromm, E. *The Art of Loving.* New York: Harper & Row, 1974.

Gazzaniga, M.S. *The Social Brain: Discovering the Networks of the Mind.* New York: Harper & Row, 1985.

Grinder, J., and R. Bandler. *Trance-formations: Neuro-Linguistic Programming & the Structure of Hypnosis.* Moab, UT: Real People Press, 1981.

Hackney, H., and S. Cormier. *Counseling Strategies and Objectives.* Englewood Cliffs, NJ: Prentice-Hall, 1979.

Hall, E.T. *The Silent Language.* New York: Doubleday, 1973.

Hallman, G.V., and J.S. Rosenbloom. *Personal Financial Planning.* New York: McGraw-Hill, 1984.

Hamilton, C., et al. *Communicating for Results: A Guide for Business & the Professions.* Belmont, CA: Wadsworth Publishing Co., 1982.

Huxley, A. *The Doors of Perception.* New York: Harper & Row, 1970.

Ivey, A.E. *Intentional Interviewing and Counseling.* Monterey, CA: Brooks-Cole Publishing Co., 1982.

Luft, J. *Of Human Interaction: The Johari Model.* Palo Alto, CA: Mayfield Publishing Co., 1969.

Mayeroff, M. *On Caring.* New York: Harper & Row, 1971.

McKay, M., et al. *Messages: The Communication Skills Book.* Oakland, CA: New Harbinger Publications, 1983.

Miller, J.G. *Living Systems.* New York: McGraw-Hill, 1978.

Pearson, J.C. *Gender and Communication.* Dubuque, IA: W.C. Brown Publishers, 1985.

Pulvino, C.J., and J.L. Lee. *Financial Counseling: Interviewing Skills.* Dubuque, IA: Kendall-Hunt Publishing Co., 1979.

Sincoff, M.Z., and R.S. Goyer. *Interviewing.* New York: Macmillan Publishing Co., 1984.

Smith, D.L., and K. Williamson. *Interpersonal Communication: Roles, Rules, Strategies & Games.* Dubuque, IA: W.C. Brown Publishers, 1985.

Stewart, C.J., and W.B. Cash. *Interviewing Principles & Practices*. Dubuque, IA: W.C. Brown Publishers, 1985.

Storms, R.J. *A Study of Verbal and Nonverbal Pacing Procedures as Methodologies for the Establishment* of Counselor-Client Rapport. Madison, WI: University of Wisconsin-Madison, 1982.

Tobin, J. and K. Feyen. *How to Make Decisions Creatively*. Sacramento, CA: Hartnell Publications, 1982.

Wilmot, W. *Dyadic Communication*. New York: Random House, 1979.

Wolvin, A., and C. Coakley. *Listening*. Dubuque, IA: W.C. Brown Publishers, 1982.

Zieg, J.K. *A Teaching Seminar with Milton H. Erickson, M.D.* New York: Bruner-Mazel, 1980.

Zunin, L., and N. Zunin. *Contact: The First Four Minutes*. New York: Ballantine Books, 1975.

Index

Q

R

S

T

U

V